Ad...
Executive Job Se...

"Today's job market can be a stressful and uncertain place. Too often, talent and hard work are not enough to keep careers on track in the face of economic and market turmoil. 'Replanting' ourselves in new opportunities is both an art and a science, and Vermonter Robert Wilson applies 20 years of career management experience to help today's job seekers succeed."

—U.S. Senator Patrick Leahy
State of Vermont

"For any executive anticipating a career change—or who is in the midst of a career shift—*Executive Job Search Handbook* is a must-have guide. What Richard Bolles' book did for job searchers in the last century, Bob Wilson's book will do for executive career strategy today."

—Janice Cantu
VP Human Resources, Springer-Verlag North America

"The description on the cover of Robert Wilson's *Executive Job Search Handbook* is clearly an understatement. This is much more than a simple how-to book on marketing oneself. 'Job search from the inside out' is the apt phrase Hinda Miller uses in her Foreword. After 35 years of reviewing books on career management, I have rarely come across one that involves the job seeker so deeply at the emotional level. The understanding of the state of mind of anyone going through this process is truly exceptional. The fact that Wilson includes remedies for people unhappy in their jobs and careers is an unexpected bonus."

—Richard Germann
SVP Quality Management, Manchester, Inc.

"Here's a must-read before you leave–or even think about leaving—your current position, regardless of how comfortable you are or how high up on the food chain. Everything you need to know to cope with change in this unpredictable job market can be found on these pages, including dozens of interactive exercises that personalize the experience for you. After reading Bob Wilson's book, I sleep better at night."

—Michael Ross
Executive Publishing and Marketing Consultant

"This is not so much a handbook as it is a GPS navigator, guiding its readers through some of the toughest territory they'll ever have to negotiate. And it doesn't miss a turn."

—David B. Opton
Founder & CEO, ExecuNet

"Career transition is a difficult, scary, high-stakes game. This book will not only help you make better decisions, but will make your journey much more rewarding, successful, and enjoyable than traveling solo. The knowledge you'll gain here is unparalleled in its scope and actionability....Like hiring a top-flight career coach without spending the thousands of dollars. Essential reading— whether you're actively looking for your next job, or your crystal ball sees another round of downsizing just ahead."

—Gary Alpert
CEO, WetFeet, Inc.

"The continuing stream of corporate acquisitions creates an extended opportunity for executives and senior management. *The Executive Job Search Handbook* provides the strategies for determining—and then locking in—'what comes next' in one's career. It also brings structure to the search—which means increased success for the managers and leaders who use it."

—Ron Gula
Chief Technical Officer, Tenable Network Security

Executive
Job Search
Handbook

All *you* need to *make your move* –
from *marketing yourself* with a
master resume to
*networking, targeting
companies*, and
negotiating the *job offer*.

by
Robert F. Wilson

CAREER
PRESS

Franklin Lakes, NJ

Copyright ©2003 by Robert F. Wilson

Exercises 1, 2, 3, 7, 8, and 12 courtesy of Janet Hollander, Copyright © Wilson McLeran, Inc.

Exercise 4 Copyright © The Marlin Company, North Haven, Conn., and the American Institute of Stress, Yonkers, N.Y. Reprinted by permission

Exercise 6 courtesy of Dr. Marvelle S. Colby, Marymount Manhattan College

EXECUTIVE JOB SEARCH HANDBOOK
EDITED AND TYPESET BY JOHN J. O'SULLIVAN
Cover design by Lu Rossman/Digi Dog Design
Printed in the U.S.A. by Book-mart Press

To order this title, please call toll-free 1-800-CAREER-1 (NJ and Canada: 201-848-0310) to order using VISA or MasterCard, or for further information on books from Career Press.

CAREER
PRESS

The Career Press, Inc., 3 Tice Road, PO Box 687,
Franklin Lakes, NJ 07417
www.careerpress.com

Library of Congress Cataloging-in-Publication Data

Wilson, Robert F.
   Executive job search handbook : all you need to make your move-from marketing yourself with a master resume to networking, targeting companies, and negotiating the job offer / by Robert F. Wilson.
      p. cm.
   Includes bibliographical references and index.
   ISBN 1-56414-662-6 (pbk.)
   1. Career changes—United States. 2. Executives—United States. 3. Job hunting—United States. 4. Résumés (Employment)—United States. I. Title.

HF5384.W55 2003
650.14—dc21   2003040920

Acknowledgments

A number of colleagues, friends, and industry executives have made significant contributions to the quality of this manuscript, as well as to its very existence. Among them are: Martha Buchanan; Mary Baswell; Dr. Marvelle S. Colby, Marymount Manhattan College; Rena Copperman; Brian Dalton; Stacey A. Farkas, Career Press; Grace Freedson's Publishing Network; Jack H. Fuller; Bill Hare; Janet Hollander; J. J. Laukaitis; Tom Moye; John J. O'Sullivan, Career Press; Sallie G. Randolph, Esq.; Marcia Shin; and Robert S. Tinnon. Sidebar selection and interview transcription courtesy of Martha Buchanan.

Contents

Foreword
by Hinda Miller

C hange is the only reality. Everything else is illusion. Sometimes change is thrust upon us when we lose a job; sometimes we are motivated to change jobs to fulfill a deep-seated need. Whatever the circumstance, we discover the tools that help us move into the real world, usually accompanied, to some extent, by a fear of the unknown.

In this timely book, Bob Wilson provides a roadmap for undertaking a process of self-examination; "job search from the inside out," as it were. By positioning each cycle of change to reconfigure an individual's life vision, Bob sets up parameters within which to answer the perennial question, "What do I want to be when I grow up?"

After 30 years' experience as an entrepreneur, division president of a Fortune 100 company, educator, corporate director, and state senator, I would argue that a successful business life is more about character, attitude, and integrity than it is about skills and business acumen. These skills and states of mind cannot be taught in the traditional sense. They can, however, be developed through personal coaching, studying, and developing a high motivation for self-knowledge.

The most important ingredient of my entrepreneurial success was the creation and implementation of finite "operating principles" centered on mutual respect and personal responsibility, which in turn guided all business decisions and interactions made by our company's upper- and middle-management teams–not just with one another, but also with the inevitable network of relationships that includes vendors, suppliers, and customers.

These operating principles speak more about how to "be" together than anything we might "do" together, and thus provide a context for both intrinsic integrity and problem-solving. Corporate culture is one of the most difficult areas to assess, but it is also one of the most important. To be successful, one's personal values must mesh with company values. It is fair to ask in any interview: "Do you have a set of core values? What are they, and how were you able to implement them in the companies where you have worked?"

What I appreciate most about this book is the honest voyage of discovery involved in any major life change, from self-examination to clear definition of goals and tactics to fulfill them. The integration of right-brain intuitive creativity and left-brain practical methodology will be essential in successfully guiding you through the reality of change and personal transformation. This book will give you the tools to help you enjoy that ride.

—Hinda Miller, *February 2003*

Hinda Miller is an entrepreneur, corporate executive, Vermont state senator, educator, and community activist. She is president of Deforest Concepts, a consulting firm specializing in small business and the promotion of women and entrepreneurship. She also serves on the advisory board of the School of Business at the University of Vermont.

Preface

*T*he *Executive Job Search Handbook* was written for executives who find themselves at one of the following three career crossroads:

- Recently fired, downsized, or laid off from their jobs.
- Holding jobs but, for one reason or another, believe they will soon be fired, downsized, or laid off.
- Hate the jobs they have, but without a plan for moving to a better job or career.

Those of you without jobs are going through a rough time—perhaps one of the roughest you will ever face. We don't pretend to have all the answers, nor will all of our suggestions and strategies be appropriate for everyone. What we can say is that nearly everything suggested is here because it was used successfully by the author (who, like many of you, was fired during a 20-year corporate career). Or it was used by a significant number of the thousand-plus individuals he has assisted during his 15 years as a corporate outplacement counselor and executive recruiter.

The way you lost your job may have nothing to do with the way you performed it. We all know about acquisitions, mergers, greed-inspired company failures, and the nasty human consequences that inevitably follow. On the other hand, perhaps you *are* responsible to some extent for being out of work. Either way, you need a regular paycheck from a job you enjoy, as quickly as you can manage it.

For some this will mean simply locating a position similar to the one you just held, perhaps in a company very much like the one you just left. For some it will mean striking off on a different career path—whether it is *slightly* different or *markedly* different—that may not yet be determined. If you are considering a relatively drastic career change, you probably will benefit from career counseling or testing beyond the scope of this book. (In this case, the suggestions in Chapter 3 for additional resources may be helpful.)

Amid a growing concern nationwide that corporate America has lost its way, many job seekers may be uneasy about employment in what they perceive as an amoral, nebulous environment. In the wake of dozens of greed-induced scandals, beginning with Enron's massive bankruptcy late in 2001, their fears seem justified. (At the time this book went to press, more than 11,000 jobs had been lost and $2 billion in pensions were gone for good.) However, there is little recourse. Boycotting companies you suspect of turpitude may keep you on the street for quite some time. And unless you are applying for an officer-level position, there will be little opportunity, before you accept an offer, to discuss aspects of your new company's decision-making process that affect its moral leanings.

Should you then forego due diligence as you research companies that interest you? Of course not. But if working for an honest company is high on your list of priorities, investigate each one thoroughly and then ask the necessary follow-up questions (see Chapter 5).

Much success as you plot your career course.

Robert F. Wilson
bobwilson@job-bridge.com
www.job-bridge.com

Pronoun/Adjective Gender Alert

My contribution to controlling the rampant use of "his or her," "his/her," "s/he," and "he/she," as well as various annoying single subject-plural pronoun combinations, has been to generally characterize *job seekers* as male and *interviewers* as female.

Chapter 1

Dealing With *Now* if You're Out of a Job

> "What the caterpillar calls the end of the world,
> the master calls a butterfly."
>
> —Richard Bach

If you are now out of a job—for whatever reason—please read on. Those of you unhappy in your present position but still drawing a paycheck, proceed directly to page 23.

If you're like most of the millions of Americans who have lost jobs and lived to tell about it, you will act in fairly predictable and understandable ways. This is not to deny you your individuality. It is to assure you that you are in good company in fighting through the strange and largely unpleasant sequence of emotions you will feel over the next several weeks or months. In 2001, 2.6 million U.S. workers lost their jobs. The level of mass employment, with 8.25 million officially out of work, was the highest since the recession of 1990-1991.

Several psychologists have developed a model categorizing job-loss stress into seven distinguishable stages, adapted from observations made in 1969 by the Swiss psychiatrist Elisabeth Kubler-Ross in her epic book *On Death and Dying*. Not everyone experiences each stage with the same level of intensity. Some may experience only four or five of the seven, or go through two or more of them simultaneously.

It is important to be aware of each stage as you experience it, and to understand that they are all just that: stages. Eventually each will come to an end. They are:

1. *Shock.* You probably don't know what hit you. More extreme cases include panic, confusion, and an inability to take positive action.

2. *Denial.* You may refuse to believe what has happened, and instead think that a terrible mistake has been made.

3. *Relief.* If your dismissal releases you from pressures building weeks or months ago, you may view your new-found "freedom" as an opportunity that would have presented itself only if you had quit instead.

4. *Anger.* Some of those recently fired fantasize about getting even with former bosses or colleagues they perceive to be responsible. Others become angry with themselves for not correcting a situation that became intolerable. Still others do both. Don't feel guilty if you're one of them.

5. *Bargaining.* Some people, in a futile and often panic-motivated attempt to "right a wrong," appeal to their employer for a second chance or possible reassignment. There is often justification for assignment to a more appropriate position elsewhere in the organization. In your case, however, the time for negotiating has irrevocably passed. In Chapter 2, I'll help you analyze what went wrong this time to better assure that there won't *be* a next time.

6. *Depression.* When the reality of the lost job finally sinks in, this emotion is almost invariably the result. It can mean anxiety, lost sleep, or even withdrawal from family and friends. (Such depression usually lasts from a few days to several weeks. If it persists longer than three or four weeks, it could be *clinical* depression, in which case it is time to call a physician.)

7. *Acceptance.* The time it takes to accept the loss of a job varies, but it will happen. Only at this point can you begin to think ahead and start to design your job-search plan. Understand, however, that if it takes longer than you anticipated to find employment, mild depression probably will appear. Knowing this may help you fight through this emotion if it recurs. (See Exercise 1, "Identifying Your Job-Loss Emotions," on page 26, to help see you through the various stages of job-loss stress.)

Dealing With Stress

There is a positive side to losing a job, incomprehensible as this may seem to you right now. In the process of reshaping your future, you'll learn a lot about yourself and likely will come out in the end a tougher and better person for it. Take advantage of this ideal opportunity.

Dr. Salvatore Maddi, a psychologist at the University of Chicago, maintains that such toughness can be developed, like a muscle, and enables individuals to cope more effectively with the experience of losing a job. Dr. Maddi calls this quality "hardiness." He first proposed the notion in a book called *The Hardy Executive,* published in 1984. Dr. Maddi defined this quality as a combination of thinking well of yourself, being curious, and believing that you can influence your own destiny. Most importantly, it means viewing life as an *adventure* rather than as a *source of comfort and security*. Dr. Maddi believes that people with low hardiness levels are emotionally dependent on the organizations for which they work. Hardy people, on the other hand, are more inner-directed and independent.

Maddi tracked managers at Illinois Bell Telephone Company for eight years in coming to his conclusions. During this time, top management directed the company's controversial divestiture from AT&T and engineered two strong early retirement pushes. He found that those who handled the stress of losing their jobs were extremely hardy. But he also found that hardiness was becoming a rarity in the corporate environment, with emphasis being placed on team play and conformity, despite evidence that hardy people (and presumably the more independent among them) make better workers. That tendency has become even more prevalent since *The Hardy Executive* was published, which has in turn has increased the tension on the relationship between hardy executives with strongly held views and the corporations that employ them. The hardier the executive, the more narrow the line to be walked if both individual and corporate objectives are to be met successfully and harmoniously.

Family Communications

If you are at home reading this, with a day or a week's distance from your dismissal, your family probably already knows what happened. If you had some indication weeks or months ago that you were in trouble, perhaps you had a chance to prepare your family to some extent. But if your family does not know about your dismissal, tell them immediately. If you are single and not close to your immediate family, contact close friends and share the experience with them.

The two characteristics you'll need most in the weeks and months ahead are energy and confidence. Not leveling with your family and friends will drain your energy and decrease your self-confidence, largely because of the increased anxiety you will tend to generate.

This is not to say that any family need be panicked unduly. The verbalizing of negative feelings can be overdone. A family needs to know—especially a one-income family—that the principal money earner has enough confidence to make this a temporary phenomenon. You need to transmit the message that it might be rough for a while, but you'll get through. That's what a family needs to hear.

Family Resentment

It's natural to expect some resentment from your spouse when a paycheck that is vital for meeting family needs no longer exists. This will be even more evident when your severance money runs out. A working spouse will likely feel that the entire financial load has been transferred onto his or her shoulders. A nonworking spouse may feel completely helpless and frustrated.

Children need extra consideration. It will be difficult for them to understand why privileges taken for granted are no longer available—especially younger ones. All of this is reasonable. The essential goal is to keep the job-loss problem manageable by keeping additional family stress to a minimum. Bring the entire family in on the problem as much as the understanding levels of the youngest children permit. This will promote a team effort and keep resentment, fear, and frustration down. Set up "wartime rules" as necessary to accommodate this new (but temporary) way of arranging family schedules. Rearranging your home life to accommodate a new, temporary, out-of-work status may necessitate such considerations as adding private office space, setting ground rules for the use of the telephone (adding a separate "business line" and voice mail will simplify life considerably), and managing your money more efficiently. For this last consideration, you should make an appointment with your accountant or financial advisor to arrange for a wide range of cash flow contingencies. (See Exercise 2: "Working Out 'Wartime Rules' for Your Family," on page 28.)

Departing Strategically

Severance Benefits

Chances are you were instructed about all severance benefits due you during your exit interview with your former employer's human resource representative. If not, go through your contract or your company handbook to find out just what you have coming to you. For example, vacation time you didn't use, as well as any vested rights in profit-sharing or pension plans, is money owed to you. If you have the option of accepting payment in either a lump sum or in installments, check with your accountant before deciding which method is best for you.

Healing Job-loss Wounds

During an 18-month job search, Harold had survived the first round of interviews more than 20 times and the second cut 13 times. He was a finalist eight times. Yet in each case another candidate was chosen. He began calling himself an "oafer," as in "I'm oafer eight."

Harold persisted. His friends nicknamed him Timex because he could "take a lickin' and keep on tickin'." Finally he landed a great job at a good company. "All's well that ends well," his friends said. "Yeah," said Harold. "You must be happy," his friends said. "Yeah," said Harold. But to himself he wondered, "Why don't I feel like a winner?"

At the end of their searches, many job seekers don't feel the sense of victory, accomplishment, and security they expected. Some, like Harold, experience nagging anxiety and self-doubt, and have trouble believing their triumph was earned fairly. "I'm not the same person I was before I spent 18 months on the bricks," Harold says quietly.

Leslie Gordon Mayer, a Philadelphia psychologist, notes that many terminations are carelessly handled, inflicting needless damage. "Employment lawyers say firings should be kept short and businesslike, but this can have a paradoxical effect: The person feels demeaned, creating a self-protective need to fight back," she says. "Self-worth plummets, even where objective analysis makes it clear the termination wasn't related to the individual's competency or personal qualities."

—Douglas B. Richardson
The Wall Street Journal

Exit Statement

Ask to see the exit statement prepared to describe your performance on the job and the circumstances under which you left the company, if such a statement customarily is written. This statement becomes part of your personnel folder and often is the basis for handling inquiries regarding your employment there. To protect the privacy of former employees, department policy in most companies mandates that inquiry responses include only:

1. Period of employment.
2. Employee's job title.
3. In some companies, employee's salary at time of departure.

Nevertheless, if an exit statement is written about you, be sure it is accurate and fair. Also find out specifically what information your ex-company customarily releases to prospective employers.

Many companies conduct exit interviews with departing executives to gather information about employee-manager relationships or other aspects of company policy that may be subject to scrutiny. Such information benefits the company, and not you. Be honest answering the interviewer's questions, but remember it is your right to "respectfully decline to answer" any question that may reflect badly on you when it is viewed later in your personnel folder

Company References

It will be useful to learn what kinds of references you are being given by your former employer. A prospective employer undoubtedly will want to know what one or more of your ex-supervisors thought of you. Some will ask questions in considerable detail, not necessarily excluding various aspects of your personal life. It's a good idea to call your ex-boss and ask how a reference check will be handled. You don't want to tamper with the truth, naturally, but you do want to be treated fairly. You also need to know what negative responses you will have to neutralize when you respond to a less-than-glowing reference check. If you had more than one boss at the company—as a result of promotion or transfer, for example—use as your references the boss or bosses with whom you got along well. (See Chapter 6 for specific advice regarding ways to prepare your references for calls from prospective employers.)

Health Insurance

You'll want to be sure your family is covered by medical and hospital insurance between jobs. If your spouse is employed and covered, transfer over to his or her group policy. If you are single or your spouse is not employed, investigate the continuation of your existing group policy.

Public Law 99-272, enacted in 1986, requires that most employers sponsoring group health plans offer terminated employees and their families the opportunity to extend their health coverage at the prevailing group rate for an additional 18 months, if necessary. Employees who qualify have 60 days from the date they lose coverage to inform

Short-Term Insurance: Viable Option Between Jobs

Most employment interviewers today look more favorably upon those who've been laid off than they used to. And there are alternatives to the COBRA plan. John Radovich, national sales director at Fortis Health, says short-term medical insurance premiums are usually one-third to one-half the amount of premiums under COBRA, because the short-term insurer takes less risk. Short-term medical insurance is often purchased by people changing jobs or in transition to a new career, or entrepreneurs starting a new business who need time to select a permanent insurance plan.

Remember that short-term insurance is available only for a limited period. If you think it will take you longer than six months to find a suitable job, then continuing your current insurance under COBRA would be a better solution.

—Margo Frey
Excerpted from the *Milwaukee Journal Sentinel*

the plan administrator that they want continuation coverage. Under this law, called the Consolidated Omnibus Budget Reconciliation Act (COBRA for short), employers enrolled in any of the 1,700,000 health plans affected must afford terminated employees with identical coverage to what they previously had. The caveat is that such coverage may cost you up to 102 percent of what it costs the employer.

If this all comes as news to you, call your former company's personnel office for details. If you can't get the information you need, contact the Pensions and Welfare Benefits Administration of the U.S. Department of Labor, which administers the law.

If for some reason you are not covered by COBRA (your ex-employer has not paid the premium for continuation coverage, for example), you'll need to choose another alternative. If you have an insurance agent you trust, ask for opinions. If not, spend a morning calling major insurance carriers represented in your area. Describe your situation and find out what they can do for you. At the very least you'll want to sign up for some high-deductible catastrophe term insurance so you won't be wiped out if a family member must be hospitalized for a major illness or accident. Get insurance to cover the essentials, and be sure the policy is renewable, to cover your maximum anticipated period of unemployment.

Unemployment Benefits

A small percentage of those without jobs refuses to apply for unemployment compensation, largely for reasons of pride. This makes sense, but it doesn't alter reality. Granted, the forms are tedious to complete, and you do have to appear at a specified time on a specified day every week, and you are accountable for a reasonable amount of job-seeking effort to qualify for your weekly check. Still, rarely will you meet an acquaintance in line and have to turn your head in embarrassment; nor is it a frequent occurrence that a rude civil service employee will try to humiliate you because of your circumstances. Yet these remain common apprehensions.

You are not on the dole. Your ex-employer contributed to the fund from which your checks will be drawn. Your work, in turn, contributed to the profits earned by that employer. Therefore, you are deserving of the checks you will receive, even though you may right now view the amounts as insignificant.

What your maximum weekly benefit is to be, and the formula used to determine that figure, vary widely. Each state has its own way of determining these figures, as well. In short, it is important to ask questions, no matter where you live. And because the appropriate documents that will permit you to file for unemployment insurance also vary from state to state, call your local unemployment office first to be sure you take the right paperwork and identification with you on your first trip.

Call today. The time it takes for this privilege to expire from your termination date *also* varies from state to state.

Cash Crunch

The well-beaten path of least resistance in dealing with a tight money situation is to duck creditors for a while, on the grounds that it will take them months to catch up with you, by which time you'll be out of your mess.

Wrong. This tactic only causes things to get more ugly—exponentially. First come the stronger dunning letters; then the phone calls, many of them quite embarrassing and insulting; then the personal visits; then the lawsuits and resulting panic.

There are ways to preserve your credit history while sparing yourself and your family further upheaval. Contrary to what you've been told or have thought, most creditors will not only respect you for confronting your fiscal problem, but almost universally will be willing to work with you on a plan that permits you to stretch out your payments in manageable fashion. When creditors don't hear from you and your checks dry up, their logical conclusion is that you intend to stiff them. Not surprisingly, they go into action the only way they know how.

No matter what your financial condition, your first step should be to put together a cash flowchart to see exactly what monies are coming in and going out each month. Formulate action plans based on finding a job in three months, six months, nine months, and 12 months. Determine what bills you must pay in full, what bills you can pay partially, and what payments you can delay. Plan with your family what you can live without or with less of. Then reduce your spending accordingly. If you own your home, make an appointment with your banker to consider contingency plans, such as reduced principal or interest-only payments, until you find a job.

For all other creditors—utilities, department stores, or finance and credit card companies—write a letter describing your situation, and propose a plan for payment.

Spreading the Word

Now that you've done everything possible to protect yourself and your family from catastrophe, contingency, and creditor, it's time to lay the groundwork that will permit some positive things to happen. This comes largely under the headings of image and efficiency. Both are crucial in crossing your job-bridge. Knowing how you are perceived, as well as how effectively you are able to make your case, are two good reasons to read Chapter 2.

If You Still Have a Job

If you're still drawing a paycheck, you're probably in one of the following two less-than-satisfactory situations:

- You're waiting to see whether you will suffer the fate of former downsized or laid off colleagues.
- You hate your job, but are unsure of next steps.

Your strategies will vary, depending on your circumstances.

Are You in Danger of Being Downsized?

Waiting for the other shoe to drop? It isn't always easy to tell whether the first wave of layoffs will be the last, even if you're given the most ironclad of assurances. It's not in the corporation's best interests, having layoff survivors writing resumes when they should be making sales calls. From top management's perspective, the less you know, the better.

But now that former colleagues, whose jobs you thought were safe, are employees no more, you need to be sure of your *own* perspective. Here's what it should be: You do what you must to protect your turf. This means leading by example and fulfilling your responsibilities to the best of your ability. Concentrate on high-priority tasks that improve your visibility and strengthen your reputation as a team player.

But it also means thinking beyond your current situation, and spending free time building bridges to your next job.

- Your reputation in the company is that of an effective leader, and if you've developed good connections in other divisions of your company, look within the corporation before you give up on it entirely. Jump on any viable opportunity (using techniques described in subsequent chapters), whether for the long-term or just to buy yourself enough time to delay a lengthy job search.

- Maintaining a full-time relationship with your current employer is out of the question, shift into second gear. Take home copies of letters and reports that will document and help update your resume with current accomplishments. Reactivate your network to get as many others working for you as possible.

If You Hate Your Job

As bad as your job may be, you're better off than those unsure how many paychecks they can expect before the next "corporate restructuring." That's the good news. But it isn't all the good news. Think first about improving your position *without* leaving the company.

Some people change not just companies but *careers* to find the perfect job. And as valid as this may be for many, for others the answer may be closer to home. Even the best jobs must be reinvented—when the company loses money, or you have continued conflict with a coworker, or when a boss leaves, for example. "All jobs require care and feeding," says Career Lab's William Frank. "So why not start right where you are? If that fails, you can always look elsewhere."

"Jobs usually fail around personal relationships," says Jeff Baer, vice president of operations for a division of First Financial Management Corporation. "If there's a problem, realize that you may be part of it. When we blame other people, we give up our freedom to control the situation."

Try to improve relationships everywhere they need improving: your boss, peers, subordinates, consultants, vendors, customers, or others. Make a more concerted effort to resolve outstanding issues. Change your attitude, if that's what is called for. Apologize. Become more assertive or less assertive—whatever it takes.

At the same time, resolving your conflict may require outside intervention. It is difficult to be objective about one's self. "Find a friend, minister, psychologist, or a career coach or counselor to serve as a sounding board," Baer says. "When you run out of ideas and things aren't working, that's the time to use a professional."

If you use up all of these options and are still reconciled to quitting, zero in on your most significant problem, or problems, in Chapter 2. Then, use the strategies described in subsequent chapters to construct your game plan.

Leaving With Class

The best way to quit is by trying to remember that former colleagues are potential clients, customers, consultants—or colleagues yet again. Here's a list to help assure that your bridge from old company to new remains structurally sound:

1. *Write a letter of resignation.* Just telling your boss that you quit is not enough. Put it in writing and hand deliver it the day you let others know your plans. Include your last day of work, and a brief statement of your plans, if appropriate. Express your gratitude for opportunities that were afforded you.

2. *Leave on good terms.* Try to make amends for residual hard feelings with other employees. Be remembered as a decent coworker and/or manager. If you can't stand the job you're leaving, keep it to yourself. You've found your solution; gloating about it helps no one. You may need this company connection one day.

3. *Finish what you've started.* Stay focused on upcoming deadlines, and pull your weight until the last day. Share the status of all unfinished work with colleagues and subordinates who need to know. Organize and catalog your files.

4. *Manage your exit interview constructively.* Answer all questions honestly, but keep negative personal comments to yourself. Focus on describing ways existing relationships can be strengthened. Emphasize your boss's positive qualities, as well as those of your peers and subordinates.

Exercise 1:

Identifying Your Job-Loss Emotions

Shock, denial, relief, anger, bargaining, depression, and acceptance—you may be experiencing one or more of these feelings right now. Complete the following exercise to help you identify where you are emotionally.

A word before you begin: Only by being completely honest in completing this exercise will you be able to form a realistic plan of action.

Directions:

Place a check mark next to those statements that express how you are feeling right now.

Shock

_____ I can't understand why they let me go.

_____ Sometimes when I think about being dismissed, my heart beats faster or I begin to hyperventilate.

_____ Since I was fired, I haven't been able to do much of anything. I seem to spend a lot of time just staring at the walls or wandering around aimlessly.

_____ I just don't know what's happening to me.

_____ I don't know what to do next.

Denial

_____ I just can't believe that I've lost my job.

_____ Don't they realize what they're doing to the operation by letting me go?

_____ Maybe my records were mixed up with somebody else's.

_____ It isn't really true. Tomorrow I'll wake up and it will all turn out to be a bad dream.

Relief

_____ I was planning to quit anyway.

_____ Finally, the pressure is off.

_____ I wish this happened months ago.

_____ This really doesn't come as a surprise.

Anger

_____ Someday I'm going to get even with those people.

_____ I'd really like to punch my boss in the nose.

_____ I'm furious with myself for letting this happen.

_____ Don't they realize what they've done to me and my family?

_____ Letting me go is unfair.

Bargaining

_____ Maybe I can talk them out of it.

_____ If I promised to take corrective action, maybe they would want to take me back.

_____ Perhaps I could transfer to another department.

_____ Maybe I could convince them to let me stay if I took a pay cut or a demotion.

Depression

_____ I just don't know if I'm going to make it.

_____ I really don't want to get up in the morning.

_____ How can I face my family and friends?

_____ I can't sleep nights.

_____ I seem to sleep all the time.

_____ I can't eat.

_____ I can't stop eating

_____ I'm beginning to drink too much.

_____ I'm afraid I'll never get over this.

Acceptance

_____ Well, it's happened and it's time to move on.

_____ I have some good ideas about how to go about finding a new job.

_____ This may be for the best.

_____ I've told my family and friends.

_____ I know what the problem is and it won't happen again.

Scoring:

Assess yourself one point for each check mark in the Shock, Denial, Relief, Anger, Bargaining, and Depression categories.

_____ Write that total on this line.

_____ Give yourself two points for each check in the Acceptance category and enter that total here.

_____ Subtract for your point total.

Scoring Key:

- **20 to 28:** You are experiencing severe emotional stress. Try to work through these feelings by talking with friends, family, or a counselor.
- **12 to 19:** You are experiencing strong feelings about the loss of your job. Again, discussions with family or a friend may be helpful.
- **5 to 11:** You're getting there. Just a little bit more to work through.
- **4 to 10:** Acceptance. You're ready to go full steam ahead. You've put this experience behind you.

•••

Take this test weekly until you work your way through the goal of acceptance.

Exercise 2:
Working Out "Wartime Rules" for Your Family

You now have a new, temporary, full-time job: looking for a job. Unless you have been given office space at your old place of business to conduct your search, you'll be working out of your home. This means you will need to change some of the ways things work at home. Use the following planner to set up an effective job-hunting base of operations.

Office Space

Where will you set up your office? You'll need a quiet space with a work surface that doesn't have to be cleaned off every evening and set up again the following day. It should also have convenient access to the phone.

I'll set up the office in _____.

I'll need to move in some furniture, namely _____

_____.

I'll need to collect some things to stock my work space.

_____ computer	_____ Organizer or PDA
_____ fax machine	_____ stapler
_____ pens and pencils	_____ calculator
_____ note pads	_____ calendar
_____ personal stationery	_____ paper clips
_____ other	
_____	_____
_____	_____
_____	_____
_____	_____

Telephone

It is important that during this time your telephone is answered in a professional manner and that you get complete messages in a timely fashion. It is also important that the telephone remain free for important incoming calls. You'll also need to set up your answering machine with an appropriate message when no one is available to take calls.

The following people in my family will be answering the phone: _____

_____.

When they answer, they'll say: "Good morning/afternoon, _____

_____."

If I'm not here, they'll say: "I'm sorry, he's not in at the moment. May I take a message?" Make sure message pads and pencils are always available near the telephone. Instruct message takers to restrict their responses to simple information, such as

"I expect her back by 3 p.m." and refrain from gratuitous details ("He's playing bridge." or "He went down to the library.").

The telephone will remain free for incoming calls between _____.

Quiet Hours

During the next few weeks, you'll be completing tasks that require concentration, such as updating your resume and writing letters. You'll need to balance your need for quiet to accomplish these tasks along with your family's need to engage in activities that make noise. So try to negotiate two to three hours of quiet time daily.

Quiet hours at our house will be _____.

Chores

As part of your financial planning, you may decide that the family will need to do some of the chores you used to hire outsiders to do, such as gardening, housecleaning, car washing, and the like.

Task	Who Will Do It	When
_____	_____	_____
_____	_____	_____
_____	_____	_____
_____	_____	_____
_____	_____	_____
_____	_____	_____
_____	_____	_____
_____	_____	_____
_____	_____	_____
_____	_____	_____

Use of Car

Does your being out of work change the transportation situation in your family? We'll work out our transportation needs by:

_____

_____

Family Meeting

Set up a specific time to have a meeting with your family to go over the "Wartime Rules."

Be clear what is expected and why, and let family members know how much you appreciate their help.

Chapter 2

Taking Advantage of Your Career Crossroads

> "Nobody can make you feel inferior without your consent."
>
> —Eleanor Roosevelt

If you have taken care of everything suggested in Chapter 1, it is now time to trace the reasons for your dismissal (if that was the case) or your sense of urgency about the possibility of losing your job, if that is the case.

But first, let's deal with those of you still on the job, but not sure that you're going to stay there, as well as those of you desperate to leave.

You didn't have any control if there was a cutback or a staff reduction brought about by an acquisition, merger, or poor financial performance. Nor were you able, if this happens to have been the case, to alter the decisions of a new boss with priorities that excluded you.

It happens all the time. For one reason or another, a manager's boss leaves, and the manager's power base goes away as well. The boss's replacement can, if so inclined, take at least two courses of action that won't do the manager a bit of good:

1. If the new boss feels sufficiently threatened by the manager, who may have been in line for the job, guess who goes on the block immediately?
2. The new boss may feel more comfortable reassembling a team that worked well together under a previous banner.

In either case, the manager is out of a job.

Identity Crisis

The number of corporations that changed their names as a result of mergers, acquisitions, and restructuring hit a record 2,976 in 2000, according to Enterprise IG, corporate "brand building" consultants. The total reflects nearly a 300-percent increase over 1983, and breaks the previous record of 2,576 set in 1999. "For a corporate name and related systems," says Enterprise IG vice president Peter Mack, "you can expect to spend between $70,000 and $100,000."

—Loretta W. Prencipe
InfoWorld

If you were just hit by one of these swinging pendulums, skip on to Chapter 3. Read on only if you were fired for inadequate performance, poor work habits, or an inability to relate well to your boss or coworkers.

•••

If you have been fired before, there may be something wrong with the way you arrive at the decision to accept a job. For example, you may not be finding out enough about what you are ultimately getting into. Perhaps you have relied more on gut instinct than on serious research. Or maybe you've been too concerned in chasing top dollar when a combination of other criteria would have resulted in greater job satisfaction.

Finally, think about this: You may have accepted a job for which you were over- or under-qualified, or not sufficiently trained. Many terminations are inevitable from the first day on the job. This is often true if you've come from a smaller company. The hiring process in larger organizations is nearly always effective enough to avoid such lapses.

It is important to consider these issues in order to realistically assess your position. In Chapter 7, we'll deal with another aspect of this decision-making process as it affects evaluating job offers.

Why You?

It's obvious that you either do or don't know why you lost your job. Or, maybe you *think* you know but aren't quite sure. The rest of this chapter will help you draw some conclusions about the reasons for your departure, so that you can begin a course of corrective action if it seems necessary. It is the first means of getting back on a positive career path.

A New Breed of CEOs

A new generation of chief executives at some of the nation's largest companies are redefining the qualities required to succeed as business leaders.

Most are still in their 40s and were influenced by very different historical and cultural forces from their 60-something predecessors. They were in elementary school when JFK was assassinated and when Martin Luther King proclaimed, "I have a dream."

They were too young to be drafted to fight in Vietnam, and some watached their older siblings go to war or join antiwar protests. They listened to Bruce Springsteen, Led Zeppelin, and other rock music, and were the first to use computers.

They started their careers in the late 1970s and early 1980s, riding the wave of Wall Street mergers and the stock-market rise that was tempered briefly by the crash of 1987. And they catapulted up the corporate ladder during the booming 1990s—several years younger than the generation before them—when new technology and the creation of many new companies promised a new age of affluence.

"These new CEOs came of age at a time of unprecedented prosperity and now they've entered an age of vulnerability," says Warren Bennis, business professor at the University of Southern California and author of *Geeks and Geezers*. This isn't what they bargained for. But they've grown up with so many choices and such affluence, they can hopefully become pathfinders."

The 40-something CEOs tend to manage from the top all the way down the ranks. They tell their employees they don't have all the answers, and prefer to listen. The new CEOs know that time in the corner office will last only as long as they show improvement.

–Carol Hymowitz
The Wall Street Journal

Before you do any serious thinking about where you went wrong, try to collect any available firsthand information about the situation. Former coworkers can give you an accurate and honest evaluation of your job performance and attitude. They can talk candidly about what they think the problem may have been. Those at your level or above are more likely to give you the straight story than those who reported to you or were at lower levels in other departments. People who used to report directly to you are the least reliable sources because they may view themselves as on the wrong end of a "blamed messenger" situation, and may equivocate or withhold information accordingly.

It is entirely possible that you were not told all the factors that led to your dismissal. That lack of information can hamper your ability to make an intelligent decision about what aspects of your professional life to change. Few firing authorities have the stomach for confronting terminees about their major flaws. Finding themselves in such situations, most bosses simply don't want to hurt others' feelings. And although you probably will have some difficulty working up much sympathy, an overwhelming majority of these people find firing an extremely painful act. Perhaps you've been on the other side and know this firsthand.

Select three to six people with whom you worked closely who know your work habits and style, but who probably didn't say a lot at the time of your departure, except to wish you well and commiserate on the "raw deal" you received. Evening calls at home are probably best, but if you find you have to call the office, pick a time when you have reason to believe each will be available to talk for a few minutes. Call an early-arriver before 9 a.m., a late-luncher just after noon, and a late-leaver after five. Here is an inquiry model you can adapt to your own style and personality:

> "Hello, Al? Gordon Cummings. Is this a good time for you to talk for a few minutes? Good. I wanted to ask you something that might be difficult to answer, but I really need you to level with me. I've been doing a lot of thinking about my career plans these days, as you might imagine, and I don't want what happened at Pebex to happen to me next time. I want to avoid making the same mistakes, even if it means a career change.

> "Here's how you can help me, Al, if you will. I want you to think back on any ways I could have improved my performance, work habits, or personal relationships that might have prevented my departure.

> "Now, if you want to think about this for a day or so and have me call back at a time good for you, that's fine. But if you have a few minutes now and some points occur to you, that's even better. The only thing I ask is that you tell it to me straight. I can take it, and I really need to know the truth—for my own sake."

Whatever you say, in whatever variation, must be said with comfort and heartfelt meaning. Remember, you are asking for honesty. You must be able to accept the comments made to you as a result without rancor or defensiveness. Just receive the information, take notes, and ask for elaboration where you need more detail or where the point is not clear. Don't argue. Some information or criticism you hear for the first time may indeed hurt. This is one reason that corroboration by at least one or more other colleagues is essential to test the accuracy of your source.

If this isn't the first time you have been fired, you might want to talk to coworkers at a previous employer's company in an effort to discover a pattern. What you learn from those who worked with you on a day-to-day basis may help you determine what went wrong.

What Do *You* Think About You?

After analyzing the results of your phone calls, there is another way to assess your suitability for the job you previously held. This is to use an adaptation of what many apprentice salesmen learn as the "Ben Franklin Close," an exercise that exemplifies the common sense closely associated with that 18th-century American genius and statesman.

Simplified for our purposes, it requires dividing a sheet of paper vertically and listing on the left-hand side all of the things you liked about your last job. Try to relate each point to your position, your function (marketing, finance, or operations, for example), your company, and your industry. Then on the right-hand side, list all of the things you didn't like doing, using the same categories. (This is all set up for you in Exercise 3, "Pluses and Minuses," on page 47.) This exercise will help you learn more about yourself and take you a step closer to determining the extent to which you want to continue in the same career field. It also will make you aware of your decision-making patterns in the jobs you historically have chosen.

There's always the possibility that you won't want to change a thing. However, be skeptical if you come to this conclusion, because it may merely indicate a deep-seated and well-disguised fear of change. On the other hand, if your firing can be identified as nothing more than a sharp personality clash between you and your ex-boss, a virtually identical workplace with a boss to whom you relate better should be satisfactory.

Now that you know more about yourself by looking at where you've been professionally, it may help to examine the categories described on the next few pages. These categories are designed to help you identify your own work style, attitudes, and state of mind. If you see yourself to a meaningful extent in one or more of these categories, consider it a cue to continue looking in the same direction.

Burnout

In the late 1970s, New York psychologist Herbert J. Freudenberger coined the term "burnout" to define mental fatigue from job tedium and stress. The affliction also can stem from frustration caused by devotion to a cause or lifestyle that has not reaped expected results.

Some people burn out because they work too long and too hard. A few other reasons include:

- Too much pressure and ambition.
- Insufficient reward for above-average accomplishment.
- Too little control.
- Unappreciative or myopic senior management regarding talent and efforts.
- Inappropriate criteria for promotion and compensation.

Here are some classic symptoms of burnout:

- Indifference to assignments, deadlines, and workload.
- Impatience with family and friends.
- Increased consumption of alcohol, food, or drugs.
- Persistent physical or mental fatigue.
- Frequent fantasies about "running away."
- Overwhelming feelings of inadequacy about both work and personal life.

A 2002 study by the federal government's National Institute for Occupational Safety and Health cites stress as a major problem in the lives of more than half of all workers in the United States—twice what it was in similar studies 10 years earlier. "People are stressed off the map," says Dr. Stephen Schoonover, author of *Your Soul at Work*, who helps executives combat stress.

Psychologist Christina Maslach has devised a test for burnout called the Maslach Burnout Inventory. Originally written to measure emotional exhaustion among members of the "helping professions" (police officers, counselors, teachers, nurses, social workers, psychiatrists, physicians, psychologists, and attorneys, among others), it is applicable to other industries and workers as well. This test must be administered by a professional trained in testing or counseling.

The American Institute of Stress, a Yonkers, New York research group, estimates that the results of stress—absenteeism, burnout, and mental health problems—cost American business more than $300 billion a year. They have devised a "Workplace Stress Scale"(less rigorous and more easily administered than the Maslach

Stress in the Workplace

- 40 percent of all U.S. workers report that their job is "very" or "extremely" stressful.
- 25 percent of all employees view their jobs as the number one stressor in their lives.

—Northwestern National Life

- 75 percent of all employees believe workers have more job stress than a generation ago.

—Princeton Survey Research Associates

- Work problems are more strongly associated with health complaints than are financial problems or family problems.

—St. Paul Fire and Marine Insurance Co.

Burnout Inventory) that will help you compare your stress level with that of American workers surveyed by telephone over a two-week period in 2001. (See Exercise 4 on pages 50.)

Plateauing

A first cousin to burnout is the concept of "plateauing," a concept thought to be popularized by psychiatrist Judith M. Bardwick, who also is president of Bardwick and Associates, an international management consulting firm. If you were passed over for promotion or prestigious assignments in the months before you were eased out, and generally felt out of the mainstream of decision making for some time before that, it may be that you had reached a plateau—or peaked to the point of sharply diminished alternatives. Plateauing doesn't lead to dismissal as frequently as does burnout, largely because an individual presumably is performing adequately in the assigned role. It does, however, clearly cut off any possibility of rising higher in the corporate pyramid. The job threat arises as a result of the frustration felt at realizing there is nowhere else to go, and ending up in nasty confrontations with the boss. Such tactics rarely succeed and frequently end with an abrupt elimination of this threat to the boss's job.

Corporate Misfit

[Note: "Misfit," as used in the following several sections, is intended to connote a *bad* fit, which mirrors the word's primary definition in most dictionaries. It is not meant to reflect on the character of any individual locked in a destructive work environment.]

A corporate culture is a powerful force, impervious to individual or group pressure to change. Corporate norms affect an individual's attitude and performance from a number of different perspectives. They occur in such areas as information sharing (it either is a norm or it isn't), innovation (it's either encouraged or it isn't), self-expression, and socializing within one's work group.

Industrial psychologists have identified two basic types of corporate culture: closed and adaptive cultures. In a "closed" corporate culture, as described in a study by Professor Ralph H. Kilmann of the University of Pittsburgh, work units guard their fiefdoms carefully and share little information. They protect themselves at all times, minimizing risks and generally exhibiting extreme caution. An "adaptive" corporate culture, on the other hand, requires both risk and trust.

Individuals who don't tune in quickly to the many nuances of their corporation's culture usually find themselves in deep trouble. Those who are patient and clever enough to go through the motions can survive until they are able to find a position with another company in which the culture is more in tune within their own work habits, attitudes, and style. Mavericks who think they can buck or change the system, however, are in for a rough time. Without compromise, their paydays definitely are numbered.

One extreme remedy that will permanently eliminate corporate cultural problems is to start a business of your own—thus creating your own corporate culture. This is not a easily made decision, and the risks are high. Nevertheless, there may be reasons for you to consider such an alternative. If the notion generally appeals to you, take your gut feeling a step further by completing Exercise 5, "Testing Your Entrepreneurial Quotient," on page 51. If you're satisfied with the results, read the boxed feature "Start Your Own Business?" on page 41 to see what you'll be getting into.

An excellent source for information on going into business for yourself is the Small Business Administration. Early in 2003, the SBA had offices in 95 cities throughout the United States, some of which conduct information-sharing seminars during the year. Check your telephone government section pages under "Small Business Administration" or "SCORE" (Service Corporation of Executives), or log on to the SBA Website: *www.sba.gov.*

Start Your Own Business?

One of the first steps in deciding whether to leave corporate life and start your own business is to take stock of your attitudes and to analyze your feelings about the changes that will occur.

Following are two checklists to help you evaluate your feelings about the benefits of autonomy, as well as its drawbacks. In the first part of the checklist put a plus sign next to the benefits that are important to you. In the second part (see page 42), put a minus sign next to the drawbacks that seriously concern you.

If the number of minus signs is greater than the number of plus signs, say consultants Robert W. Bly and Gary Blake, security is probably more important to you than autonomy, and you might be happier in a structured environment.

Benefits of Autonomy

- Make more money.
- Work when you please.
- Work at home.
- Make decisions independently.
- Be a big fish in your own pond.
- Hire employees on *your* terms.
- Enjoy flexibility of small business.
- Take risks and reap rewards.
- Save on taxes.
- Be your own boss.
- Pick your own projects.
- Be free from boredom.

Functional Misfit

Go back over your list of likes and dislikes (Exercise 5, page 51). If it seems relatively clear that you have problems identifying with the kind of work you are doing, perhaps your functional fit is all wrong.

Check first to see if there is any misalignment between your dislikes and your major responsibilities. Do people, data, or things dominate the work you have been doing? In

Start Your Own Business? (cont'd.)

Drawbacks of Autonomy

- No regular paycheck.
- Work longer hours.
- Need to raise own capital.
- No sounding boards.
- Experience loneliness.
- Absence of corporate financial resources.
- Risk personal financial loss.
- No corporate perks or benefits.
- Answer directly to clients.
- Total responsibility for running the company.
- Maintain hectic, demanding schedule.
- Sustain motivation enough to work without supervision.

other words, to use an extreme illustration, if you function in information systems and lack of people contact is prominent among your job dislikes, you might well be a functional misfit.

Still, you shouldn't conclude from this single analysis that it is time to change careers. This is merely an indicator that should cause you to investigate further. Moreover, most jobs involve people, data, *and* things, so very rarely will such an examination yield enough evidence for a final decision. Still, if you think you are on to something, spend some time in the library with the *Dictionary of Occupational Titles*. Published by the Department of Labor, the *DOT* categorizes some 20,000 jobs on the basis of whether they emphasize people, data, or things.

Much more comprehensive is John L. Holland's *The Self-Directed Search*, including his "Occupations Finder." In 20 minutes—and for $9—you can score yourself in six attitudinal areas: Realistic, Investigative, Artistic, Social, Enterprising, and Conventional. *The Self-Directed Search* (SDS) is answered, scored, profiled, and interpreted by the user against the Occupations Finder, which provides descriptive codes for nearly 500 occupations. If the results of the SDS are not conclusive, Dr. Holland and his associates have prepared a *Vocational Exploration and Insight Kit*. Though it takes the SDS a step further, it must be administered by a professional counselor or psychologist.

Industry Misfit

This one should be easiest of all to fix. If you find your job function satisfying, but the industry you're in is distasteful, boring, alien, meaningless, or nonsensical, investigate appropriate "functional memberships" in your local, state, regional, or national professional societies.

With at least one notable exception, functions travel well from industry to industry. Financial analysts, human resource directors, corporate counsels, information technology managers, media relations specialists, and purchasing agents normally can adjust fairly well from industry to industry. More often than not, it is just a matter of improving one's network to find out where the action is.

The notable exception has to do with a fundamental economy shift from manufacturing- to services-based industries. For the past two decades, this has eliminated both jobs and companies on the manufacturing side. More and more blue- *and* white-collar workers are fighting for fewer and fewer manufacturing jobs, even as an increasing number of jobs in services go unfilled.

If you find yourself in this bind, go back to the Holland *Self-Directed Search* described on the previous page, or to a qualified counselor or psychologist if the test results are inconclusive.

Managerial Misfit

All managers must learn to train, delegate, mediate, motivate, influence, encourage, evaluate, correct, and change behavior. Sometimes this must be done on the spot. When unforeseen problems surface, corrective action often has to be identified and administered immediately. The way a manager handles a sensitive employee's mistake can affect that person's performance—sometimes permanently.

In the face of such sizable responsibilities, it seems only logical that companies would spend considerable time and money training managers to be effective leaders. This happens less frequently than it should, and most men and women promoted into supervisory positions are left to manage by either common sense or instinct. Some improve their skills after a few years on the job; others never improve at all.

David McClelland, a psychologist, and David Burnham, a management consultant, teamed to produce a study of managerial styles published in *Psychology Today* some years ago. Their research revealed three clear-cut approaches to management, based solely on the personalities and apparent psychological needs of the individuals tested. As you will see, the three styles offered starkly differing degrees of effectiveness.

Good-Guy Bosses

Managers with an overwhelming need to be liked (or who are extremely afraid of being disliked) tend to be lousy bosses. They believe that a happy ship is a good ship, and that tight supervision only rocks it. Their directives and deadlines usually are vague, their criticism is rarely specific, and their response to unsatisfactory performance is often inappropriate.

A good-guy boss often makes exceptions to company rules just to keep on good terms with employees who ask for special favors. Consequently, such a boss usually alienates those workers who are trying to go by the corporate book. They see their boss's inconsistent application of the rules rendering them powerless to control their professional lives. Whether they perform well or poorly, they don't know what to expect next.

Because good-guy bosses care more about fellowship than effectiveness, they also have trouble giving critical feedback to subordinates. Fearing that they won't be liked if they give negative feedback, they either minimize it, don't offer it clearly and honestly, or don't give it at all.

McClelland and Burnham found that good guys ran fewer than 25 percent of all departments that performed "above average" under their criteria, and more than 75 percent of all departments that functioned "poorly."

Power-Trip Bosses

Managers who regard their departments or divisions as personal turf usually make good short-term bosses, but generally are ineffective over the long haul. Because they rule by fear and threat, they are obeyed. Deadlines and objectives are met.

McClelland and Burnham found, however, that most power-trip bosses do not want their subordinates to be responsible to the organization, but only to them. Because they reward only subordinates who are loyal to them personally, their long-term effectiveness is markedly diminished. Power-trip bosses tend to have high turnover in their departments. Additionally, those who report directly to them are usually reluctant to offer ideas, knowing that they will rarely, if ever, get credit for them. Thus innovation and improvement are seldom associated with power-trip bosses, unless they generate it themselves.

The Middle Road

The previous two very real (and perhaps slightly overdrawn) characterizations may bear just the faintest resemblance to a style of leadership that has caused you trouble. Still, even if you see only a little of you that needs changing, the following may be of interest.

Between the good-guy boss and the power-trip boss is room for a sizable gray area of management style that harnesses and redirects power, not for its own sake, but in a team effort toward the fulfillment of short- and long-term company objectives. McClelland and Burnham called such bosses "institutionalized-power managers." They are also called by other researchers "assertive delegators," as opposed to "nonassertive delegators" (good-guy bosses) and "aggressive delegators (power-trip bosses).

In *The Way of the Ronin,* Dr. Beverly Potter describes the boss as coach, with fairly stringent guidelines. (In feudal Japan, Ronin were samurai who left the service of their masters to make their own way in the world. With neither money nor skills, they had to live by their wits.) Her five fundamental ingredients for this kind of successful leadership, which can be found in detail in her chapter titled "Corporate Ronin," are summarized below.

1. *Tell the employee* what targets are to be reached and provide regular feedback to monitor, adjust, and redirect performance. Be concise, specific, and direct. Avoid vague guidelines ("We expect you to show initiative.") and judgmental or emotional statements ("That was a half-assed job."). Describe no more than one situation at a time.

2. *Ask for information* in order to elicit participation and develop employee potential. Probe with open-ended questions ("What are you looking for?" is better than "Are you looking for responsibility?"). Avoid "why" questions, which tend to put employees on the defensive. Ask enough questions to get all relevant information and communicate that you are listening seriously.

3. *Describe specifically* how the information and suggestions you gathered during the *"Ask"* stage will be translated into a plan of action. Indicate who will do what, under what conditions, and to what extent. Vaguely stated plans lead to problems on interpretation and accountability. Negotiate the plan with the employees. Draw upon their experience and knowledge, and encourage their commitment.

4. *Check performance frequently* so you'll be able to take quick action at the first sign of trouble. Monitor employees at different times and in varying sequences to insure that employees don't perform at their best only at check times. Use charts and graphs where possible to motivate performers at all levels. Encourage self-charting to allow employees to record and rate their own performances.

5. *Acknowledge and reinforce good* performance. Comment on specific actions. Tailor your positive feedback to the individual. Pay attention to ways in which the person is performing as desired. Encourage employees to acknowledge and reinforce one another. Likewise, encourage

self-acknowledgment, which is the cornerstone of high self-esteem, and is essential for self-starting and self-directing behavior.

Potter maintains that a Ronin management style will permit you to get the most out of your creative and autonomous subordinates. At the same time, it allows employees who lack self-direction to similarly contribute a peak performance. If you believe your management style or skills may be in question, consider testing your managerial mettle with Exercise 6 on page 54.

Behavioral Misfit

Many people have trouble adjusting to group norms. Some just don't care how they come off, while others have no idea that their personalities are abrasive, disruptive, or alienating.

There are many gradations of behavior, ranging from completely acceptable to completely unacceptable. All behavior can be judged by a myriad of values and standards.

At one extreme are the mavericks, whose highly individualized way of looking at problems, or life, can be thwarted in a corporate culture that rewards lockstep behavior and punishes anything else. That's why many mavericks border on being corporate misfits.

At the other extreme are those individuals who need psychological help, or whose behavior is otherwise influenced by domestic problems. These are situations that need attention, but that are beyond the scope of this book.

The vast middle ground is where you likely will find yourself if you suspect that an attitudinal problem played a part in your dismissal. But unfortunately, as the bad breath advertising slogan went years ago, "Even your best friends won't tell you." (See Exercise 7: "Identifying Attitude Problems," on page 60.

Outside Help

In addition to the specific suggestions made in this chapter, help and source materials are all around you, wherever you live. Check nearby community and four-year-college-sponsored workshops, public library reference sections (many have "career corners"), and local adult education offerings put together by the YMCA and other community organizations.

Now here's the generic, simplified action plan you need to keep in mind to get across your job bridge:

- Phase 1: Identify the appropriate problem category that applies to you.
- Phase 2: Develop a plan of action for overcoming the problem.
- Phase 3: Work continually to improve.

Take a half day to analyze the results of exercises in this chapter you have completed, and decide whether to dig more deeply into the one or two areas that may be possible trouble spots for you. If further counseling or testing seems a good idea, delay the work on your resume and marketing plan until you see more clearly what your course of action should be.

This becomes a tricky decision, though, for a couple of reasons. You don't want to lose a lot of impetus in getting your campaign started, but neither do you want to risk going off in a direction that will cause you to repeat some of your old mistakes. (See Exercise 8: "Problem Assessment and Action Plan" on page 62 at the end of Chapter 2.)

Exercise 3
Pluses and Minuses

Use this exercise to take a close look at what was good and what was bad about your last job. Think in terms of activities, skills, responsibilities, contact with people, or the environment.

Position (The job itself):

What I Liked	**What I Didn't Like**
_____	_____
_____	_____
_____	_____
_____	_____
_____	_____

Function (The type of work, such as accounting):

What I Liked	**What I Didn't Like**
_____	_____
_____	_____
_____	_____
_____	_____
_____	_____

Company:

What I Liked	What I Didn't Like
_____	_____
_____	_____
_____	_____
_____	_____
_____	_____

Industry:

What I Liked	What I Didn't Like
_____	_____
_____	_____
_____	_____
_____	_____
_____	_____

Other:

What I Liked	What I Didn't Like
_____	_____
_____	_____
_____	_____
_____	_____
_____	_____

Now, using what you have just written and any further thoughts you may have, complete the statements below:

At work I need: _____

_____

_____

_____

I am interested in: _____

_____

_____

_____

_____

I excel at: _____

_____

_____

_____

_____

I don't do well at: _____

_____

_____

_____

_____

I like to: _____

_____

_____

_____

I don't like to: _____

_____

_____

_____

I try to avoid: _____

_____

_____

_____

I value: _____

_____

_____

_____

Now, read over your answers and think about them.

In summary, what I've learned from this exercise about my last job is: _____

_____

_____

_____

_____

What I've learned from this exercise that may help in my next job is: _____

_____

_____

_____

_____

Exercise 4:
The Workplace Stress Scale

In terms of your current job, how often does each of the following statements describe how you feel?

	Never	Rarely	Sometimes	Often	Very Often
1. Conditions at work are unpleasant and/or sometimes even unsafe.	1	2	3	4	5
2. I feel that my job is negatively affecting my physical or emotional well-being.	1	2	3	4	5
3. I have too much work to do and/or too many unreasonable deadlines.	1	2	3	4	5
4. I find it difficult to express my opinions or feelings about my job conditions to my superiors.	1	2	3	4	5
5. I feel that my job pressures interfere with my family or personal life.	1	2	3	4	5
6. I have adequate control or input over my work duties.	1	2	3	4	5

	Never	Rarely	Sometimes	Often	Very Often
7. I receive appropriate recognition or rewards for good performance.	1	2	3	4	5
8. I am able to utilize my skills and talents to the fullest extent at work.	1	2	3	4	5

To get your score and compare your answers with others who have completed this scale, add the numbers reflecting your answers to all eight questions below.

Interpreting the Workplace Stress Scale

- Total score of 15 or less (33 percent of those completing scale): You are chilled out and relatively calm. Stress isn't much of an issue.
- Total score of 16 to 20 (35 percent of those completing scale): Fairly low. Coping should be a breeze, but you probably have a tough day now and then.
- Total score of 21 to 25 (21 percent of those completing scale): Moderate stress. Some things about your job are likely to be quite stressful, but probably not more than most.
- Total score of 26 to 30 (9 percent of those completing scale): You may be coping, but life at work can be miserable. You may be in the wrong job, and could benefit from counseling.
- Total score of 31 to 40 (2 percent of those completing scale): Stress level is potentially dangerous. You should seek professional assistance and consider a job change.

Workplace Stress Scale Scores by Demographics:

- Overall   18.4
- Men   18.6
- Women   18.1
- Ages 18-34   17.6
- Ages 35-49   19.2
- Ages 50+   18.4

Exercise 5
What's Your E.Q.? (Entrepreneurial Quotient)

Do you wonder if you could succeed as an entrepreneur? Studies of successful entrepreneurs reveal common characteristics: family backgrounds, early experiences, motivations, personality traits and behavior, and values and beliefs. How do you fit these patterns? What is *your* entrepreneurial quotient, your E.Q.?

This test can't predict your success. It can only give you an idea whether you will have a head start or a handicap to work with. Entrepreneurial skills *can* be learned. The test is intended to help you see how you compare with others who have been successful entrepreneurs, and to help you consider whether you really want to work at building your own enterprise.

	Plus	**Minus**
1. Significantly high numbers of entrepreneurs are children of first generation Americans. If your parents were immigrants, add one. If not, subtract one.	____	____
2. Successful entrepreneurs were not, as a rule, top achievers in school. If you were a top student subtract four. If not, add four.	____	____
3. Entrepreneurs were not especially enthusiastic about participating in group activities in school. If you enjoyed group activities—clubs, team sports, double dates, and so forth, subtract one. If not, add one.	____	____
4. Studies of entrepreneurs show that, as youngsters, they often preferred to be alone. Did you prefer to be alone as a youngster? If yes, add one. If no, subtract one.	____	____
5. Those who started enterprises during childhood—lemonade stands, family newspapers, or greeting card sales—or ran for elected office at school can add two. Enterprise can usually be traced to an early age. Those who did not initiate enterprises, subtract two.	____	____
6. Stubbornness as a child seems to translate into determination to do things one's own way—a hallmark of proven entrepreneurs. If you were a stubborn child (you wanted to learn the hard way), add one. If not, subtract one.	____	____
7. Caution may involve an unwillingness to take risks, a handicap for those embarking on previously uncharted territory. Were you cautious as a youngster? If so, subtract four. If not, add four.	____	____
8. If you were daring, add four more.	____	____
9. Entrepreneurs often speak of having the faith to pursue different paths despite the opinions of others. If the opinions of others matter a lot to you, subtract one. If not, add one.	____	____

	Plus	Minus

10. Being tired of a daily routine is often a precipitating factor in an entrepreneur's decision to start an enterprise. If an important motivation for starting your own enterprise would be changing your routine, add two. If not, subtract two. _____ _____

11. If you really enjoy work, are you willing to work overnight? If so, add two. If not, subtract six. _____ _____

12. If you would be willing to work "as long as it takes" with little to no sleep in order to finish a job, add four more. _____ _____

13. Entrepreneurs generally enjoy their activity so much that they move from one project to another—nonstop. When you complete a project successfully, do you immediately start another? Is so, add two. If not, subtract two. _____ _____

14. Successful entrepreneurs are willing to use their savings at the outset of a project. If you would be willing to spend your savings to start a business, add two. If not, subtract two. _____ _____

15. If you would be willing to borrow from others, too, add two more. If not, subtract two. _____ _____

16. If your business fails, will you immediately work to start another? If so, add four. If not, subtract four. _____ _____

17. If you would immediately start looking for a good paying job, subtract one more. _____ _____

18. Do you believe entrepreneurs are "risk-takers?" If so, subtract two. If not, add two. _____ _____

19. Many entrepreneurs put long-term and short-term goals in writing. If you do, add one. If you don't, subtract one. _____ _____

20. Handling cash flow can be critical to entrepreneurial success. If you believe you have more knowledge and experience with cash flow than most people, add two. If not, subtract two. _____ _____

21. Optimism can fuel the drive to press for success in uncharted waters. If you're an optimist, add two. Pessimists, subtract two. _____ _____

Scoring Key:

- 35 or more: You have everything going for you. You ought to achieve spectacular entrepreneurial success (barring acts of God or other variables beyond your control.)

- 15 to 35: Your background, skills, and talents give you excellent chances for success in your own business. You should go far.

- Zero to 15: You have a head start of ability and/or experience in running a business, and ought to be successful in opening an enterprise of your own if you apply yourself and learn the necessary skills to make it happen.

- -15 to Zero: You might be able to make a go of it if you venture out on your own, but you will have to work extra hard to compensate for a lack of built-in advantages and skills that give others a "leg up" in beginning their own businesses.

- -43 to -15: Your talents probably lie elsewhere. You ought to consider whether building your own business is what you really want to do, because you may find yourself swimming against the tide if you make the attempt. Another work arrangement—working for a company or for someone else, or developing a career in a profession or an area of technical expertise—may be far more congenial to you and allow you to enjoy an appropriate lifestyle.

Exercise 6:
"Test Your Managerial Mettle"

The following test is based on an actual case study that tracks the day-to-day challenges faced by a fairly typical manager in an East coast sportswear company.

The case consisted of a series of situations in which the manager had to make a decision or select a course of action. In this test, *you* are that manager, and you'll have to make those decisions to the best of your ability.

Each situation has four alternatives. Circle the one approach you believe is most appropriate. An analysis and point rating, as well as a scoring scale and diagnosis, appear at the end of the test.

Setting

Chris is a regional sales manager for a company that manufactures a complete line of women's sportswear. His territory: the East coast. Direct reports: 10 sales reps and an administrative assistant. Chris has been with the company for 10 years. The first six he spent as a sales rep in Tallahassee.

Right now, Chris works out of the home office with an inexperienced secretary hired four months ago. There are three other regional sales managers scattered across the country. All report to the national sales manager.

It's Monday. Chris gets to work shortly before 9 a.m. He's scheduled to make a presentation during the regular monthly sales meeting, which runs from 10 a.m. till noon.

He'll be talking about a new reporting system he's developed and field tested with his staff. Meeting attendees: Sam (the national sales manager) and the other regional sales managers.

Situation 1

These are the items in Chris's in-box: a note to call his Boston sales rep, a customer complaint about damaged merchandise, and a memo from his boss about a customer who's stopped ordering from the company. The first thing he should do is:

    a.   Dictate a reply to the dissatisfied customer.
    b.   Return the phone call to Boston; it's important territory.
    c.   Deal with his boss's memo.
    d.   Pull together his presentation for the 10 o'clock meeting.

Situation 2

The memo from Sam concerns a memo from *his* boss, the VP of sales and marketing. It reads: "Sam, I ran into George Brown, president of LaFrance department stores. He told me his buyer isn't going for our line anymore. Bad news. LaFrance is one of our biggest clients in the Tallahassee area. So please try to get to the bottom of this." Sam, who doesn't like reading *or* writing memos, writes: "Chris???" Chris's best course of action is to:

    a.   Have his secretary get the sales rep in Tallahassee on the case ASAP.
    b.   Sit on it until after the 10 o'clock meeting.
    c.   Dictate a memo to Sam explaining that the LaFrance people have always been difficult and that he has complete confidence in the Tallahassee rep.
    d.   Call the Tallahassee sales rep right away and ask him to explain why LaFrance has stopped buying and why he wasn't informed directly.

Situation 3

It's now 9:30 a.m.; the meeting is half an hour away. How should Chris fill his boss in on the action he's taken?

    a.   Outline in a memo what he's doing and what he plans to do to follow up.
    b.   Call Sam now and fill him in.
    c.   Ask Sam's secretary to relay this message: "Got your memo on LaFrance, and am working on it."
    d.   Outline in a memo what he's done and plans to do and then copy Sam's boss, who made the initial request.

Situation 4

When Chris walks into the meeting at 10, people are milling around. No one is seated yet. Sam strolls in and drops his folder at a seat in the middle of the table. Chris should:

a.   Drop his papers anywhere at the table.
b.   Put his papers down at the seat immediately to the right of Sam's.
c.   Plan to sit opposite Sam.
d.   Take a seat at the head of the table, in the position of command.

Situation 5

The meeting starts with status reports from the regional sales managers. Then Sam turns the meeting over to Chris, who introduces his proposal for a new sales report form. During a question-and-answer session, two of the regional sales managers suggest minor modifications that don't alter the form's basic format. In response, Chris should:

a.   Thank them for their contributions and turn the meeting back to Sam.
b.   Turn to Sam and comment, so the others can hear, that the new suggestions greatly improve the concept. Then ask Sam for his opinion.
c.   Politely reject the suggestions because they're not substantive.
d.   Urge others at the meeting to offer their thoughts.

Situation 6

After the meeting, Chris gets right back on the LaFrance case. He'd had just enough time before the meeting to call the Tallahassee rep and find out why the LaFrance buyer had canceled. Apparently, she feels the company's line is out of date. Chris's next step: He calls his other sales reps to get a quick rundown on how the line's been moving in their territories. Their report, in short: All's well. Chris, who had the Tallahassee territory himself for six years, knows the LaFrance buyer. His best course of action now is to:

a.   Fly to Tallahassee to see the sales rep, who is new to the territory, and possibly the LaFrance buyer.
b.   Have the sales rep fly up to the home office and talk to Chris.
c.   Have one of the other sales reps check up on the Tallahassee rep and then report back to Chris.
d.   Call the LaFrance buyer and discuss the problem.

Situation 7

Chris takes off for Tallahassee. Harry, the sales rep there, meets him at the airport decked out in a high-fashion suit and tie. There is no problem picking him out of the crowd. Tallahasseans are far less flashy, and are far more laid-back. Harry, a top-notch sales rep from New York, appears to be the wrong choice for the Tallahassee territory. Chris should:

a. Fire Harry on the spot, before the problem gets any worse. Then, Chris should pay a visit to the LaFrance store and try to save the account.

b. Advise Harry to loosen up and be less abrasive. Then give him one more quarter to clean up his act. Chris should also drop by the LaFrance store and see what he can do to salvage the account.

c. Tell Harry he's being transferred to a territory he's better suited to. Then drop by LaFrance.

d. Visit LaFrance and ask the buyer if it would help to put another rep on the account. Tell Harry nothing, yet.

Situation Analyses Score

Situation 1

C   C is the first choice. After all, it is Chris's boss who will determine his future in the company, so his memo should be first priority **(4 points)**.

B   The call to Boston can wait—at least until after the boss's memo has been handled because the sales rep didn't indicate an emergency **(2 points)**.

A   Chris can hold off on the complaint letter and still get a reply out in the afternoon mail. Also, he could check with the rep in the customer's area before responding to determine whether the merchandise was damaged in shipping or whether there was a production problem **(1 point)**.

D   If Chris has waited until now to prepare his presentation, he's waited too long **(0 points)**.

Situation 2

D   D is the best choice here. Chris needs the facts firsthand, and the rep is the obvious source. If the rep is out when Chris calls, he can leave word to have the rep call back in the afternoon. That way, a day won't be lost in telephone tag. Even better: Chris will have something to report to the boss at the 10 o'clock meeting, if Sam brings it up **(4 points)**.

B   Postponing the call may cost a day or more. If the rep is not in when Chris calls in the afternoon, there's a chance he'll have to wait until tomorrow to get the ball rolling **(1 point)**.

A   It's not a good idea to have a secretary make the call. Chris is better equipped to read the sales rep's response, not to mention that the rep might take exception to Chris's secretary being the designated interrogator **(0 points)**.

C   It's bad form to respond to the boss's memo without first getting the facts **(0 points)**.

Situation 3

C   Asking Sam's secretary to relay the message is not only the least time-consuming way to keep his boss informed, it's also the *best* way to communicate with him, considering Sam doesn't like memos **(4 points)**.

A   Because Sam dislikes memos, he'd probably regard it both a waste of his time as well as Chris's **(2 points)**.

B   With a meeting to go to in half an hour, Sam won't want to waste time chatting with Chris. His secretary will have the best sense of when to give Sam the message **(1 point)**.

D   It would be a bad move to go over the boss's head. Not only would it make Sam look bad, it might also make Chris look like a poor team player **(0 points)**.

Situation 4

B,C   Both are good choices. However, B, in Chris's case, may be a slightly better choice for the simple reason that most people are right-handed and naturally look to their right more often for advice and counsel. Seated to the right of his boss, Chris is in a better position to exert indirect control over the meeting. Sitting directly opposite Sam, (option C) is a strong alternative, because Chris could easily maintain eye contact with him. Sam will just naturally look across the table and speak directly to Chris, and vice versa **(4 points for either B or C)**.

D   This move is generally viewed as a transparent ploy for power and prestige. In Chris's case, taking the head seat would put him too far away from the boss **(1 point)**.

A   Seating shouldn't be taken lightly. In fact, the rule of thumb is that it's never wise to sit more than halfway down the table from the person in power. The closer you are, the better **(0 points)**.

Situation 5

B   This move enables Chris to publicly recognize his peers' contributions and to prod Sam into giving his seal of approval on the project. While this action may take some of the credit away from Chris, his procedure will have a better chance of being adopted and successfully implemented **(4 points)**.

A   Thanking the contributors is not enough. No one really knows how Chris feels about the ideas or whether they any of them will be implemented **(1 point)**.

C   If Chris wants their support, it would be foolish to reject their suggestions out of hand, even if he doesn't agree with them **(0 points)**.

D   If someone doesn't comment, don't force the issue. Besides putting people on the spot, soliciting comments from silent group members often elicits negative feedback **(0 points)**.

Situation 6

A   A is the best course of action here. It will be instructive to observe the sales rep's behavior and style and to see how he interacts with the people in his territory—particularly those at LaFrance. Also, if the rep hasn't been responsive and helpful, a visit to LaFrance may be just enough to salvage the account **(4 points)**.

B   Observing the sales rep in his own environment is far more revealing **(2 points)**.

D   A call—or visit—to the customer at this point may be premature. It would make more sense to talk to the sales rep first **(1 point)**.

C   A good sales rep will resent being used as a company spy. Besides, the Tallahassee rep's performance is Chris's responsibility **(0 points)**.

Situation 7

B,C   Both B and C are good choices. If Chris feels he can coach Harry, he may want to go with option B and keep him in Tallahassee. If he feels there is little room for change, then he should go with option C and try to relocate him to another part of the country as soon as possible **(4 points for either B or C)**.

A   Firing Harry means losing a good sales rep who is simply in the wrong territory **(1 point)**.

D   A manager should be making these kinds of difficult decisions—not a customer. This kind of action would not only reflect badly on Chris, it would make the customer wonder about doing business with the company again **(0 points)**.

Scoring Key

- **23-28: Outstanding.** You have an excellent grasp of how to monitor and grade your staff.
- **17-22: Very good.** But there's room for improvement. You may want to invest a little more time analyzing ways you deal with your staff and peers.
- **11-16: Okay.** But you may want to work at becoming more diplomatic. Start by replaying a recent confrontation with a peer, subordinate, or client; then think about what you might have done to avoid the conflict.

- **Under 10: Not okay.** You can't rely on your current management style. Make a concerted effort to bone up on the basics of planning and directing the performance of your staff.

Exercise 7:
Identifying Attitude Problems

Your attitude inevitably affects the way you interact with people and the way they perceive you. A "poor attitude," as defined by your boss, may be a cause of losing your job.

Look through the attitudinal categories below and check those behaviors that apply to you. Try to be as honest and objective as you can when you evaluate your attitude.

Indifference

Do you show a lack of interest for others' concerns or feelings? On your last job, did you:

_____   Find your mind wandering when others were talking to you?

_____   Continue what you were doing when someone came in to talk to you?

_____   Fail to make and keep eye contact when others were speaking?

_____   Fail to identify with the point of view of the person speaking to you?

_____   Frequently interrupt colleagues before they finish?

I'm Better Than You

Do your actions give the impression that you think you're superior to others? On your last job, did you:

_____   Tell people often that they were wrong or that they didn't know what they were doing?

_____   Consistently point out the mistakes of others?

_____   Consistently point out your accomplishments to others?

_____   Fail to treat others with respect?

_____   Belittle others for backgrounds "beneath" yours?

Kick Me

Do you "ask for" the abuse you get? On your last job, did you:

_____   Preface many of your remarks with self-deprecating phrases like, "I'm probably wrong here, but…"?

_____ Find yourself bringing up issues you knew would be shot down even when you could have kept quiet?

_____ Use a whining tone of voice?

Let It All Hang Out

In an effort to be straightforward, do you share inappropriate information? On your last job, did you:

_____ Tell your colleagues about your personal life in excessive detail?

_____ Listen to and pass on personal and company gossip?

_____ Spend company time dealing with your personal life, particularly over the phone?

_____ Tell people exactly how you feel about others?

Ain't It Awful

Do you complain frequently? On your last job, did you:

_____ Complain about how unfair the company was?

_____ Complain about the people you had to work with?

_____ Complain about your spouse/children to your coworkers?

_____ Tell others that you "weren't understood"?

_____ Feel that the world was out to get you?

Introvert

Do you fail to communicate as much as you should? On your last job, did you:

_____ See yourself as a shy person?

_____ Often know what to say, but fail to say it?

_____ Avoid talking with others when possible?

_____ Close your door or avoid eye contact with passersby?

The Lone Ranger

Do you see yourself as different from everyone you worked with? On your last job, did you:

_____ Often hold the unpopular view?

_____ Often go ahead on your own without following company procedures?

_____ Refuse to give up, even after a decision went against you?

_____ Promote your view aggressively?

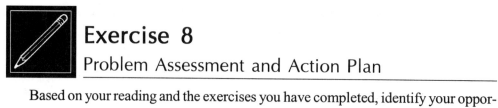

Exercise 8
Problem Assessment and Action Plan

Based on your reading and the exercises you have completed, identify your opportunities for change.

_____	My problem is burnout.
_____	My problem is function-related.
_____	My problem is industry-related.
_____	My problem is related to my managerial skills.
_____	My problem is behavior-related.

Now is the time to make a plan for change. The first step is to state your goal. The most effective goals are stated specifically within a definite time frame. For an industry-related problem, "I will identify and investigate career opportunities in three related industries on or before June 15," is much more effectively stated, than "I will investigate other industries."

Once you have listed your goals, the next step is to think of activities that will help you accomplish that goal. It is also helpful to come up with obstacles that may prevent you from reaching your goal, as well as possible strategies for overcoming them.

Use the form on this and the next page to complete your action plan.

Problem Area: _____

My Goal(s): _____

_____

_____

_____

_____

_____

_____

_____

_____

_____

_____

_____

Activities	Who Can Help Me	Completion Date	Possible Obstacles/Solutions
1.			
2.			
3.			
4.			
5.			
6.			
7.			
8.			
9.			
10.			
11.			
12.			
13.			
14.			
15.			
16.			
17.			

Chapter 3

Developing an Action Plan

> "If we don't change, we don't grow.
> If we don't grow, we are not really living.
> Growth demands a temporary surrender of security"
> —Gail Sheehy

So here you are at a career crossroads, with a number of ways to go: straight ahead, sharply left or right, or taking a less dramatic turn involving fewer risks. (Even if you were fired, laid off, or just want to gracefully remove yourself from an untenable situation, retreating is not an option.)

Now that you've identified your principal problem area or areas, you can use this new self-knowledge to upgrade your job search. What is easiest, and perhaps most productive, is to continue on a career path similar to your previous one, after correcting any flaws that put you in one of the misfit categories described in Chapter 2. In your field, you know the people, language, risks, and rewards. This is the way to go if the work still excites you, and could make you glad to confront familiar challenges that are meaningful to you.

Testing the Waters

Maybe, just maybe, this is the time to explore the career you always wanted, but for whatever reason weren't willing to risk failure. Or, you were afraid you would suffer several years of low pay until you made it happen. Perhaps, you didn't wish to deal with

Switching Industries—A Viable Option?

According to John Challenger, CEO of the outplacement firm Challenger Gray & Christmas, 56 percent of his clients found jobs in new industries in the fourth quarter of 2001—the highest level in 10 years. Challenger says that functional experience—sales or finance or IT or human resources—is often more critical than the industry you work in: "Most people have skills that are very portable."

Switching industries isn't easy. In-house recruiters and headhunters often screen out applicants without industry experience. Steve Zales, CEO of Spencer Stuart's Talent Network, reports that only 10 to 15 percent of his clients will consider someone from outside the industry for middle or upper management.

The key to any industry crossover is being able to package your skills and talents in a way that your target industry can appreciate. Networking will take you the rest of the way (for specific tips, see Chapter 5).

If such a switch appeals to you and is an option, here are a few industries to consider:

- *Healthcare:* Everything from hospitals and clinics to Big Pharma and biotech.
- *Government:* By 2005, 45 percent of senior execs working for Uncle Sam are expected to retire, according to the General Accounting Office.
- *Education:* With more than 2 million teachers projected to retire by 2008, school systems are relaxing some requirements to encourage mid-career converts.
- *Construction:* Low interest rates have helped anything housing-related, such as mortgage banking, to stay surprisingly strong despite the slowdown.
- *Security:* This field is growing, for obvious reasons. In information technology, security is the new thing. It's so hot that the industry is scurrying to develop certification standards.
- *Insurance:* Recruiter Tom Rowe of Korn/Ferry says that this field was experiencing a major talent upgrade even before recent events made it suddenly irrelevant.

—Anne Harrington
Excerpted from *Fortune*

the ridicule of family and friends who judged such a direction whimsical at best, ludicrous at worst.

Following are the stories of three Baby Boomers who realized before it was too late that their fate was in their own hands. When they were sure of their goals, they pursued them single-mindedly without looking back.

Building Contractor to Family Doctor

In 1981, at the age of 33, Dan Austin was a building and electrical contractor in northern Idaho. Dan's wife, Sandy was a teacher, and about to give birth to their first child. For a number of months Dan had shared with Sandy a vague sense of dissatisfaction—that perhaps he could be doing more for humanity than building houses.

"I was thinking I could be a family physician," says Dan. "I knew I had the intellectual capacity, but I had no idea what doors would be open or shut, or how I'd respond to being back in school as a new dad—not to mention all the financial hardships that would follow."

After high school, Dan earned a degree in math, started a career teaching middle school, and married Sandy, a fellow teacher. Five years later, feeling the pull of the western wilderness, he and Sandy quit their teaching jobs, sold their house, and moved to Sand Point, Idaho. She found a new teaching job. He started a construction business, building and rehabilitating houses. After a few years, Dan questioned what he was doing with his life.

Encouraged by the family doctor who delivered his daughter, Dan signed up at Whitworth College, 75 miles west in Spokane, as a fifth-year grad student with an eye toward meeting premed requirements.

A few medical schools he applied to after finishing premed thought this middle-aged guy must be purely on a lark, but once the admissions people interviewed him they realized how serious he was. At Dartmouth Medical School in New Hampshire, Sandy taught while Dan studied. Tuition from federal health education loans helped, as well as the Dartmouth scholarship fund. Still, he ended up about $60,000 in debt.

Dan's first day as a practicing family doctor was September 3, 1991, his daughter's 10th birthday—and 10 years to the day after the decision to leave Idaho.

"I'm a guy who loves to do it all," Dr. Austin says. "I look back and wonder why it took me so long. But once I figured it out, I was never surer about anything. I see some guys who are only 30 and burned out. I just turned 48 and *feel* 30."

Woodworker to Biomedical Engineer

As a child, David Greene's favorite past-time was woodworking. In the years since then, he has found a way to use his manual dexterity to help others, and profoundly affect their lives, as well. In his words:

The common thread throughout my life's choices has been my love of working with my hands. I always enjoyed building things and collecting tools, even if it interfered with schoolwork!

When I graduated from high school, I enrolled at the University of Pennsylvania in a pre-veterinarian curriculum with a biology major. Eventually, I became disenchanted and dropped out.

I apprenticed with a cabinetmaker for a year or so, and then decided to start out on my own. My perfectionist nature got the better of me before long. I would estimate a job, then keep reworking it until I liked it, by which time I had dissipated any profit there might have been.

Through a series of coincidences, along with some family pressure, I returned to Penn, this time intending to become a dentist. One day, working out in the gym, I overheard two people talking about research they were doing—implanting materials in rabbits to test their compatibility for later use in humans.

I struck up a conversation with them, which eventually led to a research project from the Department of Orthopedics at the university hospital. Through it, I built six instruments for use in hip replacement operations, two of which were totally new. This led me to a biomedical engineering major, and a job when I graduated—with the orthopedic division of Pfizer pharmaceuticals. One of my innovations is used in every knee prosthesis sold today.

A couple of years later, my family dentist convinced me that through dentistry I could merge my artistic and creative abilities, *and* help people. So I applied to Harvard Dental School, and was accepted in the spring of 1978.

Today I specialize in the correction of jaw and facial deformities, the treatment of growth abnormalities, and dental implants. I've changed a lot of people's lives for the better, which is very gratifying. I also have some time for a little woodworking on the side—and that's also a good feeling.

•••

Both Dan Austin and David Greene were motivated to change careers by a fundamental dissatisfaction with their professional lives. For both, such a profound change took several years to accomplish. Both spent a considerable amount of money, including tuition and fees for additional education, not to mention the loss of income while they attended classes full-time. But the commitment to change in both instances was so

Where the Jobs Are

If you're thinking of changing careers, you should know that some areas are hotter than others. The Federal Bureau of Labor Statistics projects significant growth in the following 16 professions between now and 2010. For more job-search information by industry, profession, or state, view the BLS Website at: *www.bls.gov/oco/cg/home.htm*

Projected Growth by Profession, 2000-2010

- Computer software engineers: 95 percent.
- Computer support specialists: 97 percent.
- Desktop publishers: 67 percent.
- Systems analysts, computer scientists, and database administrators: 62 percent.
- Medical records and health information technicians: 49 percent.
- Public relations specialists: 36 percent.
- Advertising, marketing, promotions, and sales managers: 32 percent.
- Biomedical engineers: 31 percent.
- Financial analysts and personal financial advisors: 29 percent.
- Management analysts: 29 percent.
- Environmental engineers: 26 percent.
- Television, video, and film camera operators and editors: 26 percent.
- Computer hardware engineers: 25 percent.
- Economists and market and survey researchers: 25 percent.
- Environmental scientists and geoscientists: 21 percent.

Net Gain in Jobs by Metropolitan Area, 2003

- Los Angeles: 94,800
- Washington: 86,700
- Boston: 83,800
- Atlanta: 69,800
- Houston: 69,400
- Chicago: 68,600
- Phoenix: 61,200
- Dallas: 57,700
- New York: 51,000
- Detroit: 41,000

—Occupational Outlook Handbook, 2002-2003
U.S. Department of Labor Bureau of Labor Statistics

powerful that they were able to move forward, regardless of the substantial obstacles that could have distracted them.

Many others who change careers, however, do so out of necessity. Bill Hare is one of them.

Investment Banker to Website Developer

In 1997, at the age of 36, Bill Hare retired from a high-paying investment banking job in Manhattan. He was fed up with 100-hour work weeks and the grind of living in the big city. In 14 years, he had saved enough to say goodbye to banking forever, and live off his investment income. Or so he thought.

For the first couple of years after retirement, Bill lived the good life. First, he and his brother James moved to the Florida Keys for a year of fly-fishing, sea kayaking, and snorkeling. Then he rode his bicycle across the country, from Oregon to Connecticut. And he traveled all over the world—to Tasmania, Portugal, Easter Island, Guatemala, and Bora Bora.

Late in 2000, Bill settled down in the mountains of northwestern New Mexico, a stone's throw from a great fly-fishing stream. His travel bug was sated, and he thought he might settle down, get married, raise some kids in the clear air of the Rockies, perhaps even write a book or a screenplay. He didn't *need* to work, because his life savings were cleverly invested in NASDAQ's high technology stocks. The Internet company stocks were changing the world, and they only went up. He even taught himself to build Websites, to better understand the products of the companies he invested in.

Then came the crash.

Over the next 18 months, Bill's savings evaporated. Like tens of thousands of others, he thought at first he could wait out the downturn. "Markets always recover," said the experts. But the U.S. economy was stuck in a deep rut. Investment banks were laying off thousands, so he couldn't return to his old life even if he wanted to. He needed to earn a living again, but had no idea what to do. What he did know was that he wanted to live in the country, be his own boss, and do something socially responsible if possible.

In the summer of 2002, at the invitation of a friend, Bill put his belongings in storage and moved to Copan, a small town in the highlands of Honduras renowned for its ancient Mayan ruins. This would be a good place to clear his head and lick his (self-inflicted) wounds. He started taking Spanish classes. He got to know the locals.

One day, the owner of a nearby eco-tourism business mentioned that she wished she had a Website. Flavia owned a sizable plot of land, but had virtually no cash. She believed a Website would bring more visitors to her eco-hacienda.

The impoverished people living on Flavia's land were cutting down the forest at an alarming rate, burning the trees for fuel. She needed money to plant seedlings of a

Think With Your Gut

To researchers who study how managers think, the most brilliant decisions seem to come from intuition. A growing body of data from economics, neurology, and cognitive psychology suggests that instinct, or hunch, or "learning without awareness" is a real form of knowledge. People who make decisions for a living are coming to realize that in complex or chaotic situations—for example in today's brutally competitive business environment—intuition usually beats rational analysis. And as science looks closer, it is coming to see that intuition is not a gift, but a skill that can be learned. Here are two guidelines for honing your instincts:

Practice, practice: This is the most important thing. "Gut instinct is basically a form of pattern recognition," says Howard Gardner, a Harvard professor and psychologist. The more you practice, the more patterns you intuitively recognize. List decisions you've made that turned out right; list mistakes too. Then reconstruct the thinking. Where did intuition come in? Was it right or wrong? Are there patterns? Highly intuitive people often let themselves be talked out of good ideas. "Generally you're better with either people or things," says Manhattan psychologist and executive coach Dee Soder. If you're intuitively gifted about people, write down your first impressions of new colleagues, customers, and so on. You want to hold onto those gut reactions.

Breed "gut thinkers: "Dismantle the obstacles that prevent people from using their guts. High turnover rates are inimical to developing the deep expertise that hones intuition. Because gut feelings are inherently hard to express, don't let people jump on a dissenter who hesitantly says, "I'm not sure...." Instead, say "Tell us more." Some leaders go around the table twice at meetings to give people a chance to put hunches into words. To sharpen your intuitive thinking, you have to get out of your own way. To foster it among those around you, you have to get out of their way, too.

—Thomas A. Stewart
Excerpted from *Business 2.0*

fast-growing fuel-wood that would relieve the pressure on the rare native trees. An increased cash flow would ensure that this small corner of Honduras would have an ecologically sustainable economy.

With his laptop and digital camera, Bill spent the next few days taking photos and writing text. Soon, Flavia had a simple Website. When Bill showed it to her, she cried. To her struggling eco-hacienda, a Website meant that her business and her forest would survive—perhaps even thrive.

A week later, the owner of the Spanish school that Bill was attending heard about the Website he had built, and called him into her office. Despite his broken Spanish, Bill understood that the school wanted to waive his tuition (about $1,100) if he built them a site, too. The income the school's 12 teachers received helped their poor families significantly. But without a Website, few travelers to Central America knew the school even existed. So Bill built their site, and when he presented it to the teachers a few days later, they cried, too.

In the United States, Websites rarely bring people to tears. What was different in Copan? After talking to other locals and doing some online research about the Internet and the travel business, Bill learned that more than 80 percent of the travelers to Latin America research their trips on English-language Websites. Also, the majority of ecotourism businesses in Latin America don't have Websites, because they cost too much and are too complicated to build.

Bill's business provides low-cost, easy-to-maintain, English-language or bilingual Websites to Latin American eco-tourism companies. He believes that a vibrant and growing eco-tourism industry will help to develop sustainable economies in the third world. He now has a bilingual Website himself (*www.confluencio.com*) and began marketing his services in November, 2002. Bill plans to tour several Central American countries soon, to introduce his product in person. (His Spanish has improved dramatically now that his financial well-being depends on it.)

The same Internet that destroyed Bill's savings and independence may now not only rebuild his life, but also help a lot of other people—as well as trees—in the process. So, these days Bill Hare commutes from his bedroom to his living room, turns on his computer, and tries to make someone else cry.

Getting Help With a Career Change

It isn't necessary to go it alone when considering a career change. This is too important a decision to make without resolving doubts you may have about taking such a plunge. If all of your research and gut instincts still leave you ambiguous, get help.

Learn More About Yourself

Several testing instruments are available that may tell you how suited you are for a career direction you are considering. You can obtain tests for preferences, skill sets, and personality. They also may be helpful in a decision you are trying to make between two or more careers. The Keirsey Temperament Sorter is one such instrument. It is based on, but more comprehensive than, the Myers-Briggs Type Indicator. (Developed just after World War II by Isabel Briggs Myers and her mother, Katharine Briggs, the MBTI adopted the framework and ideas of Swiss Psychoanalyst, Carl Jung.) The Temperament Sorter is grounded on a supposition that people differ from one another in fundamental ways, and that these differences are central to nearly every aspect of their lives. These differences include the careers they select and to which they are best suited. Dr. David Keirsey, its developer, asserts that neither the Sorter nor Myers-Briggs's work is intended to definitively assign individuals to specific occupations. Rather, it simply provides a framework for further investigation. Your answers to 70 questions will determine into which of four divergent personality types you fall, and consequently what specific professions will likely be rewarding, enjoyable, and consistent with what you find most important.

The four types break down as follows:

- **Artisans** want to be where the action is. They seek out adventure and excel in any of the arts: fine arts, such as painting and sculpting; performing arts, such as music and dance; and also athletic, military, political, mechanical, and industrial arts. Artisans pride themselves on being unconventional, bold, and spontaneous. They are excitable, trust their impulses, prize freedom, and dream of mastering appropriate performance or craft skills. They seem right at home with tools, instruments, and vehicles of all kinds. Their actions are usually at getting them where they want to go as quickly as possible. Artisans represent 35 to 40 percent of the population, and break down into four types: Composers, Crafters, Performers, and Promoters.

- **Guardians** are practical and down to earth. They believe in following the rules and cooperating with others. They take pride in being dependable and trustworthy. They sometimes worry that respect for authority, even a fundamental sense of right and wrong, is being lost. Guardians have natural talents for managing goods and services—from supervision to maintenance and supply. They are meticulous about schedules, have a sharp sense for proper procedure, and are cautious about change, even though they know some change can be healthy. Guardians make up as much as 40 to 45 percent of the population, and fall into four types: Inspectors, Protectors, Providers, and Supervisors.

- **Rationals** have a problem-solving temperament, particularly if the problem has ties to the many complex systems that make up the world around us. Rationals tend to be pragmatic, skeptical, self-contained, and focused on systems analysis. They pride themselves on being ingenious, independent, and strong-willed. They are often seen as cold and distant, but this usually is the absorbed concentration they give to whatever problem they happen to be working on. Because of their drive to unlock the secrets of nature, they have done much to shape our world. Rationals are very scarce, comprising as little as 5 to 7 percent of the population. The four types of rationals are Architects, Field Marshals, Inventors, and Masterminds.

- **Idealists** are passionately concerned with personal growth and development. They are highly ethical in their actions, and hold themselves to a strict standard of personal integrity. Idealists dream of creating harmonious and caring personal relations. They have a unique talent for helping people get along with each other. The practical world is only a starting place for Idealists; they believe that life is filled with possibilities waiting to be realized, rich with meanings calling out to be understood. Idealists make up no more than 8 to 10 percent of the population, but their ability to inspire people with their enthusiasm and idealism has given them influence far beyond their numbers. The four types of Idealists are Healers, Counselors, Champions, and Teachers.

•••

For any one of the 16 areas surveyed (four basic temperaments, each with four variations), Keirsey's 10-page Career Report lists and describes for consideration 15 to 20 occupations consistent with that sub-temperament. Another nine-page report analyzes your specific character type description, by the criteria used to chart your temperament (introversion/extraversion; sensation/intuition; feeling/thinking; judgment/perception). Taking the Temperament Sorter is free. Copies of the follow-up reports are $19.95 and $14.95 respectively. (For more information, visit: *www.advisorteam.com*.)

Schools for Career Changers

Scattered throughout the country are a variety of community colleges, technical colleges, and small universities that welcome career changers who also happen to be professionally employed. At some schools, students can complete a nationally accredited M.B.A. program over a two-year period by attending weekend classes. Investigate local opportunities that may be appropriate for careers you have been researching.

Find a Coach

If you have identified the personality traits that lead you toward specific professions (as well as away from them) but *still* lack a specific direction, you may want to consider using a coach to take you the rest of the way. Thousands of coaches advise job seekers nationwide. How do you decide which coach is right for you? Asking for referrals is one way. A coach's reputation is only as good as past clients and customers say it is. Another way is to use a certified coach. Here again, referrals are advisable.

The leading association for certifying coaches is the International Coach Federation, currently including 5,000 certified members in 36 countries. The ICF's rigorous ethical standards set a high standard for the industry. For a complete description of its

Working for a Nonprofit

What's it like working in the nonprofit sector? The following positives and negatives are normally associated with nonprofit organizations. Some are double-edged swords—they function as both positives and negatives.

Positives

1. *Rewarding work.* Many nonprofit organizations have a positive impact on the health and welfare of people. They do good works that are compatible with the religious and social values of individuals who want to help others and become involved in improving their communities. People who seek meaningful work find that nonprofits provide an excellent job fit. They enable many people to pursue their passions in well-focused work environments.

2. *Interesting work.* Arts, cultural, historical, community, educational, social services, and professional organizations engage in some of today's most important work. Many of their missions center on pressing social and political issues. If you want to change the attitudes and behaviors of individuals, groups, and communities, you'll find many nonprofits to be ideal employers.

3. *Positive work environments.* Some of the most caring and selfless people work for nonprofit organizations. Many of these organizations also hire very bright and well-educated people who contribute to a stimulating work environment. If you like working with such people—especially those who share your values—then this might be the right work environment for you.

4. *Easy entry and valuable experience.* Nonprofits offer excellent opportunities for acquiring work experience. It is often easier to acquire entry-level positions with nonprofit organizations than with government agencies and businesses. Nonprofits also offer a large number of volunteer and internship experiences. Recent college graduates and women reentering the workforce often find nonprofit organizations to be more responsive to their job search than government agencies and businesses.

5. *Career advancement.* Many nonprofit jobs lead to career advancement within the nonprofit sector. This often involves moving from small to larger nonprofit organizations. Nonprofits also are excellent stepping stones for acquiring jobs in government and business.

Working for a Nonprofit (cont'd.)

Negatives

1. *Low pay.* Constrained by limited financial resources, many nonprofit organizations offer below-average salaries. Comparable jobs paying $40,000 a year in government or business may only pay $25,000 to $30,000 with a nonprofit organization. The rewards are primarily non-monetary with nonprofits.

2. *Limited career advancement.* Because many nonprofits are small organizations, your career within such an organization may plateau quickly. Career advancement requires leaving a small nonprofit organization for a higher level job in a larger nonprofit organization. If you are unwilling to seek employment with larger nonprofits headquartered in the larger metropolitan areas, don't expect rapid advancement.

3. *Stressful work environments.* Some nonprofits are highly political and bureaucratic. Others have notorious reputations for administrative incompetence and disorganization; lack quality personnel and staff development; or operate with antiquated equipment. If you prize strong leadership, clear decision points, high levels of efficiency, and the latest office technology, many nonprofits will disappoint you.

4. *Lack of accountability.* Unlike a business that measures its performance with bottom-line results, few nonprofits have similar performance indicators. They operate processes, which may or may not be directly related to specific performance and outcomes. Like government agencies, nonprofit organizations have annual budgets that they must spend. Only a few nonprofits have clear mission statements that guide their performance and hold them accountable.

5. *Uncertain financial future.* By definition, most nonprofits depend on a variety of unstable funds: from membership fees, public donations, and corporate sponsorships to foundation grants, government contracts, and commercial activities. Such unpredictable revenue streams fluctuate from year to year, and can create anxiety among employees, generate job insecurity and affect motivation.

—Ron Krannich, Ph.D. and Caryl Krannich, Ph.D.

Excerpted from *Jobs and Careers With Non-Profit Organizations,* 1999 services and certification requirements, view the International Coach Federation Website: *www.coachfederation.org*.

The ICF also offers a no-cost coach referral service, permitting interested individuals to identify and select coaches best suited for their specific situation. The organization recommends that before selecting a coach, you: a) educate yourself about coaching; b) know your objectives; and c) interview at least three coaches before you decide–asking for two or more references from each. The process for finding the right coach includes describing your specific need; specifying your ideal coach's specialties, backgrounds, and methods; establishing a fee range; and defining the scope of your search.

"It's extremely important that people be clear about what they're looking for," says Cindy Reinhardt, ICF master certified coach and founder-director of Creative Resources Group, in Ransom Canyon, Texas. "Some people know they're in the wrong career, and need a process for discovering what the new career should be. Others are simply stuck on a career path and need a breakthrough allowing them to be more successful in the same career.

"A good coach works strategically with both kinds of problems," says Reinhardt, also a founding member of the International Federation of Coaches. "Simultaneously she will explore with clients exactly what they need but are not getting in their careers; what values they hold but are not able to express. When any of us makes a move to a new career–or marriage, for that matter, or *any* major life decision–without understanding what our contribution and responsibility is to what is not working, we carry that mindset to whatever we do next, and so repeat the cycle.

"To a considerable extent, coaching is about breaking cycles. We need to be sure that when the flush of finding a new career fades, the client doesn't find himself back in the same place. When we know the change is permanent, not only are our clients fulfilled, but we are fulfilled." (For more information about Creative Resources Group, see *www.successzone.com*.)

Chapter 4

Resumes and Cover Letters

> "I have made this letter longer than usual because I lack the time to make it short."
>
> —Blaise Pascal

The resume is a multipurpose tool, critical to your job search. Together with a well thought-out cover letter, it is the document that will generate the interviews that in turn lead to job offers. Here is what a good resume should do:

- Act as an announcement that lets employers know you are available.
- Serve as a professional brochure, to be distributed among friends and acquaintances for reference and evaluation.
- Transmit the way you see yourself to a prospective employer through its content, form, and style.
- Provide a current record of your professional accomplishments, skills, promotions, and career highlights.

There is one more important role a resume plays. It is less tangible and more subtle than those mentioned above, but no less significant. The process of researching, developing, and refining one's most important professional accomplishments in an effective way can be a tremendous confidence builder.

With all of these important responsibilities, a resume clearly needs to be prepared with considerable care. All its pieces must relate to one another in seamless fashion, taking utmost care with what has gone before and what lies ahead. To reach this level of quality, be prepared to write several drafts, working as a master chef might, in reducing a multi-ingredient liquid to a fine sauce.

Omit Needless Words

> "Vigorous writing is concise. A sentence should contain no unnecessary words, a paragraph no unnecessary sentences, for the same reason that a drawing should have no unnecessary lines and a machine no unnecessary parts. This requires not that the writer make all his sentences short, or that he avoid all detail and treat his subjects only in outline, but that every word tell."
>
> —William Strunk, Jr.
> *The Elements of Style*

"Omit needless words," wrote William Strunk in *The Elements of Style*. Strunk's Book is a classic primer on writing and grammar that first appeared in *The New Yorker* magazine in 1957. It is still available today. Strunk's advice is especially true for resumes.

A resume must communicate completely and instantly. For example, if you learn about a job opening from a newspaper advertisement, there may be hundreds of other interested applicants. With this volume of response, company "first readers" (the executives doing the hiring rarely go through incoming applications) find themselves reading to *exclude* rather than *include* potential candidates.

If a division president needs to hire a new vice president of finance, readers in the human resources department may be instructed to look for five essential qualifications. If these qualities appear somewhere in the resume but are not immediately identified, out goes the resume. In such situations, 30 seconds may be as much time as an applicant has to make the first cut.

This means that the various elements a potential employer is looking for (upward mobility, tangible accomplishments, stability, and the like) must pop out and catch the reader's eye. You can accomplish this by the creative use of typefaces and white space.

By using boldface and italics, or putting key words or phrases in capital letters—all done in a systematic, consistent way—different elements of a resume can be made more visible. Similarly, by putting a little "air" between entries, or spacing some kinds of data horizontally or vertically from others, all of the elements can be made easier to read, and more data can be taken in at a single reading. For example, two- to four-line entries are far easier to read than dense paragraphs of eight to 10 lines of type, and are therefore far more likely to *get* read.

Organizing Your Resume

There are dozens of ways to write a resume. Check your local bookstore and you'll find 10 or more experts dispensing contradictory advice on the arcane art of resume preparation. Some writers advise not using resumes at all. The advice that follows is based on a survey of corporate executives and human resource directors several years ago, and updated for this book. The original survey was subsequently used by a New York career counseling firm to guide their clients in resume construction. The interviewers themselves were interviewed. Here is a capsulized version of the survey results, broken down into three categories: content, clarity, and style. (Suggestions for preparing electronically generated resumes are treated separately on page 89.)

Content

- Position yourself to enable the reader to identify both your short-term and long-term goals.
- Describe each job specifically, quantifying your accomplishments where applicable (time saved, money earned or saved, and problems solved).
- Load the resume in favor of accomplishments, skills, and responsibilities linked specifically to the job you are seeking. Eliminate excessive personal data and overly detailed descriptions of previous jobs.
- Be truthful about problem areas such as employment gaps and perceived job-hopping, but avoid including gratuitous information that may damage you.
- Always include career-related volunteer experience.

Clarity

- Limit all descriptions of jobs and accomplishments to four lines.
- Word your "objective" and "summary" sections clearly and specifically.
- Double check to eliminate errors or inconsistencies in grammar or punctuation. Ask an English teacher, local newspaper editor, or desktop-publisher friend for help or referrals.
- State your job history in reverse chronological order, making sure several positions for the same employer are not mistaken for individual employers.
- If you have more than three years of professional experience, the "Education" section should appear at the end of your resume.

Appearance

- If your design skills are average or below-average, pay a professional for a polished, tasteful look.

Department of Dishonorable Degrees

Twice a year, Jude M. Werra, of Jude M. Werra & Associates, a headhunting firm in Brookfield, Wisconsin, reviews the hundreds of resumes he has seen in the previous six months and condenses them into a single statistic. "It's the number of people who've misrepresented their education divided by the number of people whose education we checked," Werra explained. In short, the percentage of people who "invented" a degree. Werra calls it the "Liars Index." The index, which has been published since 1995, was at its highest in the first half of 2000: 23.3 percent. It now stands at 11.2 percent.

Werra, who has been in the business of "retained executive searches" for 25 years, used to interview candidates first and then do a background check. Now he checks first and interviews later, ever since an engaging interviewee said that they had been contemporaries at Marquette University in the mid-1960s. The man claimed to remember their graduation ceremony. Werra said, "I was talking about how President Johnson's daughter had attended, and about all the security, the metal detectors, and how the place was ringed with police and Secret Service and so on, and he was saying, 'Yeah, yeah, wasn't it amazing?' And he had never been there, of course."

—Ian Parker

Excerpted from *The New Yorker*

- Choose paper of good weight and quality, standard size (8 1/2 x 11), and conservative color.
- Limit your resume to two pages, if possible.
- Take any measures necessary to eliminate typographical errors, including paying an expert to check it over.

Resume Formats

There are basically only two types of resumes: chronological and functional. If you decide to go to a professional resume writer, or if resume writing is included in any career counseling you contract for, you should know how to recognize these two basic types and be aware of the advantages and disadvantages of each.

The chronological resume is structured job by job, company by company. It begins with the present and works backward in time, with all accomplishments and skills tied closely to specific employers and positions. The functional resume, on the other hand, categorizes accomplishments and skills regardless of company as a one-page professional profile. A short job history usually follows, but it generally includes only the names of the companies, job titles, and the time spent at each company.

For all its good intentions, the functional resume has one basic problem: It appears to be hiding something. Why, a reader will ask, is the applicant trying to avoid any association of jobs and duties, companies and accomplishments? Right or wrong, a sneaking suspicion begins to surface that a functional resume is being used to mask lateral or descending career moves, career changes and double changes, or job hopping.

If that perception is accurate, then a resume is likely the wrong tool anyway. If the perception is inaccurate and there is nothing or very little to hide, then a functional resume will close more doors than it will open.

There is, as usual, an ideal solution that represents a middle ground. Construct a chronological resume with a brief professional profile up top, which will position you effectively.

Targeting

Good writers write for specific audiences. Resume writers do likewise. Owners of very small companies and start-ups usually are quite interested in candidates with strengths in more than one function. In almost all other situations, a single, all-purpose resume will appeal to very few readers. If you intend to cross over in terms of industry or function, as well as consider opportunities in the industry or function you just left, you'll need to prepare a second or even a third resume.

No matter who you are writing for, the point is to address your reader's specific needs. To do this, you have to communicate three essential levels of information:

1. *Knowledge of the industry.* If you want to re-enter the marketplace at or above the position you just left, you need to demonstrate an awareness of industry trends, problems, and promise, including all state-of-the-job responsibilities you have held, along with the accomplishments that accompanied them.
2. *Knowledge of the company.* Your knowledge at the company level usually can be demonstrated in terms of the company you just left. If you are changing very little in terms of your career, a number of similarities will emerge between your last company and your next one. Your knowledge of other companies will be obvious in the cover letters you write to contact these firms.

3.   *Knowledge of the position.* If you intend to move up a notch, your knowledge of position will depend a lot on how well you absorbed the basics of the job your last boss held. In this case you need to demonstrate in your resume and cover letter that the transition will be fluid and seamless. If you are changing functions, industries, or both, it will be tougher. However, the strategy remains the same.

Putting together the best possible resume requires that you assemble all the professional, personal, and educational data that are relevant.

Components of the Resume

The Objective

After identifying yourself by name, home and e-mail address, and phone numbers, let your readers know *specifically* what job you are after. This entry, called the "*objective*" sets the tone for the entire resume. Every word written will be read with the perspective provided by the objective and the summary.

If you can, describe your ideal position in a single title. For example:

> Objective: Corporate Counsel
>
> Objective: Director of Public Affairs
>
> Objective: Chief Financial Officer, Educational Institution

Some functions vary from company to company and the titles that describe them need to be conveyed more generally:

> Objective: Publishing Senior Management
>
> Objective: Corporate Telecommunications Operations
>
> Objective: Director, Interactive Marketing

Write your objective broadly enough to encompass the position you are after—if it is called something different from company to company—but stay as focused as possible to permit your reader to see where you're going. Don't generalize to appeal to a wider range of possibilities; instead, write additional versions of your resume to reflect different opportunities you are considering. To help you write the best objective, see Exercise 9 on page 92.

The Summary

While the objective tells the reader exactly what it is you want to do, the summary tells the reader, in very specific terms, why you are qualified to do it. (It is also often called the "career highlights" or "professional profile" section.) The summary should distill your professional experience down to three to six powerful sentences that emphasize your skills, accomplishments, and any special qualifications that position you for the objective written just above it.

The summary is your opportunity to pull out all the stops. For example, an accomplishment you are extremely proud of but which took place three jobs ago can be mentioned in this section. On a "traditional" resume, such a feat may appear somewhere in the middle of page two and never get read—especially if your resume is in the hands of a first reader, giving the resume only a quick scan.

To construct your summary, review your career to date and list all of the responsibilities, achievements, and skills you believe will qualify you for your next position. Eliminate or combine any major overlaps, and begin to group your qualifications by category. Rewrite this combined list, knocking out all unnecessary words and phrases. If you have a slight career change in mind, remember that the language you use in your resume is as important as the message you are trying to convey.

Here are two examples. The first is for a financial and operations executive in an educational setting; the second is that of an aerospace technology executive:

SUMMARY OF QUALIFICATIONS

More than 30 years financial and operations management experience in the education sector. Visionary leader comfortable addressing details of budgetary constraints, as well as long-range planning issues. Demonstrated ability to assess risk and respond appropriately. Proficient troubleshooter in such disparate areas as real estate management, food service delivery, fiduciary obligations, transportation, and physical plant. Work effectively with other department heads (that is, Development Admissions, Studies, and Student Directors) to assist in meeting departmental goals and implement the organization's mission.

or...

EXECUTIVE PROFILE

Results-driven professional with extensive experience leading people and project teams, implementing full lifecycle of technology programs, and administering multimillion-dollar budgets. Seventeen years successful planning and directing activities that provide innovative information technology, business process, and customer service solutions. Respected aerospace, defense, and government services leader with established contacts in the industry.

If the terminology of your old career is different from that of your new one, discard it. Prospective employers usually see very little crossover value in skills and achievements attained in another industry or function. It is important to eliminate from your resume the language of your old industry—or even any *references* to it.

On Writing Well

"Writing is hard work. A clear sentence is no accident. Very few sentences come out right the first time, or even the third time. Remember this as a consolation in moments of despair. If you find that writing is hard, it is because it *is* hard. It's one of the hardest things that people do."

—William Zinsser
On Writing Well

If you like your work, but are looking for a position with greater responsibility (and not likely to get it in your current job) you may not need both an objective and a summary. A well written "experience" section (see the following section), in combination with an objective that serves as a positioning statement, will be just as effective and consume fewer words. For example:

OBJECTIVE

A position that allows me to continue to develop my editorial management skills and knowledge of educational publishing to create exciting products of high value.

or...

CAREER OBJECTIVE

Satellite controller specializing in real-time command and control operations, ground system troubleshooting, and procedural development.

or...

Objective: Senior marketing executive position to include strategic marketing assessment and development, marketing plan creation and implementation.

Experience

The substance of any chronologically organized resume is the body of entries devoted to specific jobs held. Many people think that a simple job description is enough. But it is more important to record how well you performed in each position.

You need to describe major responsibilities, but concentrate even more on accomplishments you legitimately own. This will give you information from which to frame a powerful, achievement-oriented experience section. Describe past achievements consistent with your present career direction, and spend as few words as possible on previous positions that have no bearing on the kind of job you are after today. Similarly, devote more attention to current or recent career-related positions than on those held years ago. Don't appear to be dwelling in the past. If you attained major goals early in your career as well as recently, load them in your current experience and keep the past relatively spare.

An exception to this is if you are returning to a career abandoned years ago. In this case, list early positions, responsibilities, and accomplishments under a resume heading such as "Relevant Experience" and try to use the entire first page describing this part of your background. That way, your objective and summary will be followed by a description of the experience that backs up your intentions. The only possible drawback to this strategy is that employment dates for the job experience you're describing may go back a decade or more. You can handle this with a footnote following the dates, such as: "For current experience, see page 2."

Accomplishments should be broken up into pieces small enough for the interviewer to spot and absorb quickly. The interviewee, on the other hand, should view each entry as the basis for a leading question about which he has rehearsed responses of from 10 seconds to 10 minutes, depending on interviewer's interest.

Think of your resume as a script for you and the interviewer. This is particularly true of the experience section. Each entry is a cue to be picked up by the interviewer as her interest dictates, and singled out for further questions if it relates to the available position.

For that reason, it is extremely important not only to include your most impressive achievements, but also to list them in order of importance from point of view of the open position. (Think of the way you wrote a topic outline in your first composition course.) Where you can, quantify an accomplishment to further appeal to the reader's interest, and follow every main point with appropriate sub-points. Here's an example:

Responsible for all sales, marketing, and positioning issues for Calcutex. During my tenure, revenues increased from $3 million to more than $12 million.

- Created new corporate identity and collateral materials.
- Initiated annual research service concept; closed more than 30 percent of all service sales in 2002 and 2003.
- Managed seminars and created seminar proceedings as additional product line.
- Managed more than 30 sales, marketing, and editorial personnel.

The most important point to remember in writing and laying out this section is: Make all key aspects of every entry as clear and as visible as possible. This will help your

The Right Word

"The difference between the right word and the almost right word is the difference between lightning and the lightning bug."

—Mark Twain

reader to take in your strengths at a single glance, and select for more careful reading those qualities that relate most closely to the target position. The layout of your resume is as important as its content (see Exercise 10 on pages 95).

Other Personal Data

Education

Start with your most advanced degree. List the name and location of your school, your major and the year you graduated (unless you're 50 or older and feel that age will be a problem). Also, include any scholarships and honors you received, as well as your grade point average (if it was notable) and relevant internships.

List any career-related extracurricular activities, along with all career-related not-for-credit courses and professional seminars you've completed, be they company-paid or not. Include all licenses and certifications that are career-related, as well as those that add a measure of boldness (such as a pilot's license) or a thirst for vigorous activity indicating a high-energy level (such as a SCUBA certification).

Miscellaneous Considerations

Here are a few personal opinions on whether you should include several frequently seen resume embellishments:

- *Career-related hobbies*: Yes.
- *Marital status, weight, height*: No.
- *State of health*: No (the all-purpose "excellent" doesn't tell a reader much).
- *Photograph*: No.
- *"References available on request"*: No (This is not your decision; when they're needed, you'll be asked for them.).
- *Military*: Include only career-related assignments or education.

Formatting an Online Resume

The elegant, watermarked, 20-pound ivory-tinted paper you used for your standard resume will be of little use when you apply for a job electronically—be it directly to a company, a recruiter, or to career-oriented portals and search engines. Your hardcopy version is not obsolete. (You'll need to save enough copies for use in interviews and networking.) However, to compete successfully in the Internet job hunt you'll need at least one more version. It must be tailored and formatted for online job opportunities, where a prospective employer, recruiter, or online job service will see it.

Electronic resumes can be submitted in several different ways: via e-mail or online in either an ASCII file or a scannable format. If you e-mail your resume, remember that most e-mail programs wrap anything longer than 72 characters over to the next line. However, there's another consideration. Let's say your resume makes it to the desk of a divisional vice president in a company that interests you. She likes your background, but isn't the person you need to talk to. So she forwards it to the chief financial officer who is the one looking for the controller (whom you think should be you). If your resume is written to 72-character lines, the last word of many of them will roll over to the next line because of the ">" followed by a space that signifies forwarded copy in an e-mail. (Multiply this by two more characters you'll lose per line every additional time your resume is forwarded.) So keep your line length to 64 characters or so to avoid an amateurish and distracting appearance.

Submit e-mail resumes as part of the message rather than as an attachment, unless you are requested to do otherwise. Many companies are spooked by attachments of any kind, and employees are instructed not to open them unless the sender is known and expected.

ASCII Text

ASCII is a common text language that allows different word processing applications to read and display the same information. ASCII, which stands for "American Standard Code for Information Interchange," describes files that are stored in clear text format. It is the simplest form of electronic text. It is not platform- or application-specific.

Because ASCII text does not recognize special formatting commands (margins, tabs, font size, and so forth), there is little need to think about white space or other stylistic niceties—or even the modest use of such typographic devices as bullets, underlines, and italics. Here are a few other rules to remember:

- Avoid using special characters, such as mathematical symbols, they will not be accurately transferred.

- Do not use tabs, for the same reason. Use the space bar instead.
- The default alignment for ASCII is left justification. To indent a sentence or center a heading, use the space bar.
- Do not use the word wrap feature when typing your resume; instead, use hard carriage returns to insert line breaks.
- Because fonts become whatever your computer uses as its default typeface and size, boldface, italics, and sizes other than the default size will not be recognized.
- Always put your name in the subject line of the e-mail. For example:
  - "Resume from John Doe"
  - "Inquiry from John Doe"
  - "Follow-up from John Doe"
  - "Thank You from John Doe"
- Use your name in the title of any e-mail attachments. For example, "John Doe Resume.doc," not "Resume.doc"

Scannable Resumes

To get read online, scannable resumes have to pass the OCR (optical character recognition) test. Those of you with scanners can translate what you've written in a way that allows the computer to read and understand it. (The resume is scanned into the system, and the computer then reads it.) There are also a few rules specific to scannable resumes:

- Typeface should be between 10 and 12 points. *The Executive Job Search Handbook* is set in 11.5 point Times New Roman type.)
- Use a sans-serif rather than a serif typeface. A serif is the tail at the end of parts of some letters—as in the "feet" at the bottom of a capital A. Sans serif (without serifs) is cleaner and easier for a scanner to read than a serif face. Examples of serif typefaces are Optima, Univers, Futura, and Helvetica.
- Boldface type and words in capital letters are okay for section headings and emphasis, as long as the letters don't touch each other.
- Stay away from underlining and italics. They may not scan accurately.
- If you use bullets, include a space after each.
- Avoid brackets, parentheses, and compressed lines of type.
- Avoid tabs and hard carriage returns whenever possible.
- Use keywords to list all your skills and strengths (these are nouns, rather than verbs). Scanners search resumes for keywords and then file them under the appropriate categories. For example, those of you with backgrounds in information technology are used to listing all the hardware, software, and platforms with which you are familiar (which may be grouped just under your objective and summary). Use multiple synonyms for the same skills to be sure

your qualifications are picked up. If you are in the fields of new media or desktop publishing, you should work in those keywords that best capture your strengths.

Type your name at the top of the page. Then, on their own lines, add your address in the standard format, followed by your phone and fax numbers. Section headings should be boldface or capitalized. Keep copies of your more polished-looking print resume for interviewers, after your electronic resume has done its job—to get you the interview in the first place. For a few examples of the final product, see pages 172-173.

Your Master Cover Letter

You'll need a basic cover letter format for each of several kinds of situations that you can personalize from instance to instance. Letters should *never* look as if they've been mass produced. If they do, it will guarantee that your resume will see the bottom of a wastebasket before it gets read.

Here are the situations for which you'll want to develop cover letters:

- Responses to newspaper or trade journal ads.
- Introductions to executive recruiters.
- Applications to corporations or institutions.
- "Cold call" presentation letters representing a career change.

Notice that the four letters reproduced on pages 166-169 for each of the situations listed above contain four elements, regardless of the circumstances for which they were written. These elements are attention, interest, conviction, and action.

Attention

It is essential to grab your reader immediately to assure that the rest of the letter gets read. This needn't be gimmicky; you might just state your business in as straightforward and as powerful a way as you can. You might rely on a news peg, perhaps a new development within the firm to which you are writing that triggered your letter in the first place (for example, a new product line or a significant earnings increase).

Interest

In this section, you'll need to describe, in hard-hitting fashion, those qualities that you believe will merit the reader's interest. Naturally, these qualities should fulfill the implied need in the *attention* paragraph.

Conviction

Now it's time to lay it on, to corroborate your pitch with one or two accomplishments that relate as closely as possible to the job you are applying for. Build your case, in terms as strong as you can make them. Note that the *interest* and *conviction* sections are in some instances interchangeable because their purpose is similar. They may be combined occasionally rather than presented in separate paragraphs.

Action

A good cover letter needs to move the reader to action. In all of the sample cover letters on pages 166-169, except the one written in response to an advertisement, notice that the writer requests an interview. By additionally indicating that you intend to call in person to ask for that interview, you increase your chances of getting it. One reason is that a reader who *knows* a call is coming will be more likely to deal with the matter in some way, even if it is only to tell an administrative assistant to screen that call. By making the call, you eliminate the possibility of a "passive" rejection. The reader is forced to deal with you, whether positively or negatively, rather than doom your letter to perpetual in-box indecision (see Exercise 11 on page 98).

Exercise 9
Writing Your Resume:
The Objective and the Summary

There is a collection of sample resumes and letters designed to help you expedite your marketing plan on pages 169-173. Read all of the specimens carefully, regardless of whether they were written for your industry or for others. You'll find words, phrases, or design ideas you might use in ways you hadn't anticipated. The point is that numerous viable alternatives exist for creating a successful marketing plan. Take the best for your own reasons, either directly or adapted as your needs dictate.

Objective

The objective should mirror the position you're after, either by specific title or by a brief generic description.

Write your objective draft here: _____

_____

_____

_____

Look at your objective carefully to make sure it will be absolutely clear to the reader. What are the principal duties required for the position listed in your objective?

1. _____
2. _____
3. _____
4. _____
5. _____

What abilities or skills will be needed for someone to be successful in the position listed in your objective?

1. _____
2. _____
3. _____
4. _____
5. _____

Now write your final objective: _____

_____
_____
_____
_____

Summary

The objective tells what you are looking for; the summary (or "professional profile," or "summary of qualifications") tells why you're qualified to do it.

Using the previous information, answer the following questions. Thinking in terms of the type of position you are seeking, what significant accomplishments highlighted your last two or three positions?

Position # 1

Title: _____

Overall Duties

1. _____
2. _____
3. _____

4. _____

5. _____

Significant Achievements

What did you do? _____

_____

_____

_____

_____

What were the results? _____

_____

_____

_____

_____

What abilities or skills were required? _____

_____

_____

_____

_____

(Repeat on a separate sheet of paper for all previous jobs.)

•••

Now go back and circle those duties, accomplishments, and abilities that relate most closely to the position listed in your objective. Your goal is to make the best fit possible between the prospective job and your qualifications. Use only those accomplishments that relate specifically to the position you are seeking.

Using the circled items, write the summary of your qualifications for the position. For maximum effectiveness, your summary should be no longer than five or six sentences.

First Draft:

_____

_____

_____

_____

_____

Second Draft:

_____

_____

_____

_____

_____

Finishing Up

Look at what you've written:

- Is it interesting?
- Is it clear?
- Is it the right length?
- Are the ideas linked logically?
- Have you eliminated all unnecessary words?

Write as many additional drafts as necessary until you are satisfied with the result.

Exercise 10

Writing Your Resume:
Employment History and Accomplishments

Start with your most recent position and list every job you have had since you left school. (If your last year of school was three years ago or less, list all the jobs held that had anything to do with your intended career.) Account for all gaps in time between jobs. If you have held more than one position with the same company, use a separate entry to detail each position.

Position #1

Firm _____ City_____

State _____

Type of business _____Annual sales _____

No. of employees ____

Supervisor's title _____

Reason for leaving _____

_____

Last title _____

From _____ To _____ Last salary $_____

Starting title _____

From _____ To _____ Starting salary $ _____

Job description _____

_____

_____

What did you like best about this job? _____

_____

_____

_____

     Think of all the problems you faced on the job that you were able to solve to some satisfaction. Briefly describe the problem, the actions you took to solve or alleviate it, and the results that were achieved. Specifically mention, for example, any situations or conditions you helped to improve, dollars you helped the firm save or earn, any of your ideas that were adopted by the firm, or ways in which you increased sales or profits.

Problem:_____

_____

_____

Action: _____

_____

_____

Results: _____

_____

_____

Problem:_____

_____

_____

Action: _____

_____

_____

Results: _____
_____
_____
_____

Problem: _____
_____
_____
_____

Action: _____
_____
_____
_____

Results: _____
_____
_____
_____

Problem: _____
_____
_____
_____

Action: _____
_____
_____
_____

Results: _____
_____
_____
_____

•••

Repeat for previous positions.

Exercise 11
Writing Your Master Cover Letter

As previously mentioned, the four essential elements of the cover letter are attention, interest, conviction, and action. Take the following notes and refer to them as you tailor cover letters for each specific job. Look at the sample letters on pages 166-169.

1. Attention

Write and refine two or three ways you might capture the reader's attention. (Hint: One good way is to refer to a prospective employer's need.)

A._____

_____

_____

_____

B._____

_____

_____

_____

C._____

_____

_____

_____

2. Interest

Write and refine two or three ways you can answer the question: "Why should the employer be interested in me?" (Hint: Emphasize your strong qualities as they relate to the employer's specific needs.)

A._____

_____

_____

_____

B._____

_____

_____

_____

C._____
_____
_____
_____

3. Conviction

Choose one or two accomplishments to demonstrate the strength of your experience. (Hint: You'll need to change these for each letter you send, to make them fit the respective situation as closely as possible.)

A._____
_____
_____
_____

B._____
_____
_____
_____

C._____
_____
_____
_____

4. Action.

Write and refine your closing paragraph. (Hint: Don't leave it up to the prospective employer to call you.)

_____
_____
_____
_____
_____
_____
_____
_____
_____

By having done your homework, you're now ready to respond effectively to employment opportunities, and can generate your own.

Chapter 5

Marketing Brand *You*

> "Life is like a game of cards.
> The hand that is dealt you represents determinism.
> The way you play it is free will."
> —Jawaharlal Nehru

Now that your electronic and hardcopy paperwork is ready to go, there are a number of ways to get the word out that you exist and are available. However, in today's competitive marketplace, you need an edge. You need a tactical plan that will assure both smooth and effective introductions to people who can help. Four of the most effective methods are described on the next few pages. These are:

- Contacting target companies.
- Contacting recruitment firms and job sites.
- Contacting online job-search portals.
- Networking and information interviewing.

Direct Contact With Targeted Companies

If you are positioned, ready to move, and know what companies you want most to work for, learn as much as you can about each of them. Start with their Websites. This will give you relatively thorough information about goods, services, mission statements, corporate culture, and key officers. But because the Website serves as an online brochure, it presents the company's best face. You'll have to look elsewhere for the warts. Here are a few good sources:

CEOs Today Value Values

When Mattel CEO Bob Eckert meets prospective managers at his company, he recalls how he was interviewed before landing his first management job at Kraft Foods 25 years ago, fresh out of school.

After meetings with a number of lower-ranking executives, Eckert was ushered into the corner office of now-retired Kraft president Ridgway Keith, expecting the usual grilling about business school grades and work experience. Instead, Keith asked him about his parents and what it was like growing up in Elmhurst, Illinois.

"It was more chitchat than a formal interview," says Eckert. "But later I realized he was asking me about my values and trying to figure out whether I would fit in with Kraft's culture."

Eckert rose to become president at Kraft before being named Mattel's chief executive officer in 2000. "Now, when I talk to young M.B.A.s and college students, I never ask about jobs on their resumes. I try to understand their values, what is most important to them, and whether they will fit here," he says.

—Carol Hymowitz
The Wall Street Journal

Hoover's Online (www.hoovers.com)

Hoover's Online is a premier online information resource for businesspeople, offering free information, along with an in-depth index available through basic or enterprise-wide business subscriptions. Its 3 million users include corporate executives, sales and marketing professionals, recruiters, business development managers, and job seekers. At the core of Hoover's Online is a database of some 65,000 public and private enterprises worldwide and the industries in which they operate. (Hoover's offers 30 days of free access to any student with an ".edu" e-mail suffix. Individual subscriptions are available for $29.95 per month and $199.95 per year.)

bizjournals.com (www.bizjournals.com)

If you are relocating, are sure of your destination, and it happens to be one of the 40 largest U.S. cities, you can get a jump on business information with a one-year subscription to that city's weekly newspaper. This Website is dedicated to the most complete, up-to-date business news. Annual subscriptions range from $52 (Birmingham, AL) to $86 (Kansas City, MO).

CompaniesOnline (www.companiesonline.com)

For a list of target companies hiring people in your specialty, along with all basic information, this is a good source. Click "computers and software" after accessing the site. This option includes 10 categories (such as data processing, information storage and retrieval, maintenance and repair, programming services, system integration, and so forth). Pick your favorite. For the sake of example, let's say you chose "computer data processing," which, on one particular day, led to the identification of 4,851 companies. The downside to this site is that entries are randomly entered and are neither alphabetized nor classified by state. If you are interested in a single location, it could be a time-consuming process.

DirectEmployers (www.directemployers.com)

The high cost of doing business with Monster.com (which early in 2003 charged employers $305 for a single 60-day job posting—double what they charged a few years ago) and other job boards, has driven a group of individual companies to form their own non-profit service. Some post only a quarter or so of available jobs on the big boards, and the rest on their own corporate sites. DirectEmployers also has a link to the National Association of Colleges and Employers (*www.naceweb.org*), which offers job posting, a resume database, interview-scheduling, with additional tools to be added.

•••

As you compile research about your target companies, look carefully for information about new developments, be they acquisitions, product lines, or reorganization specifics. These may be useful in writing an effective cover letter to accompany your resume or to fortify your interviews with company officers.

Recruitment Firms and Internet Job Sites

Online recruiting, a $780 million business in 2001, is expected to grow to $2.3 billion by 2005, according to Forrester Research. Most of this growth is expected to come from companies new to online recruitment, particularly small and mid-size companies that make up the bulk of employers.

Dozens of Internet sites specialize in job search, recruitment, career change, and vocational counseling. Some maintain relationships with the corporate world and are clearinghouses for resumes sent in for open positions.

The following Internet addresses include sites in all four of these categories. Familiarize yourself with as many sites as are helpful to you. (Experiment to learn how to get around in them, and examine their apparent success ratio for your specific professional objectives.) Register with any that provide the kind of information and services you need.

www.hotjobs.com	*www.kforce.com*
www.6figurejobs.com	*www.careermosaic.com*
jobs.internet.com	*www.vault.com*
www.theworksite.com	*www.headhunter.com*
www.wetfeet.com	*www.craiglist.com*
www.monster.com	*www.jobsonline.com*
www.flipdog.com	*www.careerbuilder.com*
www.dice.com	*www.nettemps.com*
www.brassring.com	*www.jobtrack.com*

Function and Industry Websites

As the job market continues to dry up in many areas, professional associations for a number of functions and industries are offering their members additional services, among them career counseling, special clinics for selected stages of job search, and online job listings. If you don't find your specialty in the list below, use a search engine such as Google to lead you to it.

- Association for Finance Professionals: *www.afponline.org*
- CPA Career Center: *www.cpa2bizcareers.com*
- American College of Healthcare Executives: *www.ache.org*
- Sales & Marketing Executives-International: *www.smei.org*
- American Chemical Society: *www.acs.org*
- American Society of Mechanical Engineers: *www.asme.org*

Resume Distribution Companies

Expect to pay about $100 per company for this service. Some are better than others. If headhunters are allowed to fill out a profile of the kinds of resumes they're looking for, you may get your money's worth. These details include the candidate's area of specialization, years of experience, industry, and geographical area. Peter Weddle, author of *Weddle's Job-Seeker's Guide to Employment Web Sites 2002 (www.weddles.com)* recommends Resume Zapper (*www.resumezapper.com*), ResumExpress (*www.resumexpress.com*), and Resume Agent (*www.resumeagent.com*).

Advice from the Pros

Despite recent cutbacks in recruiting departments, most job seekers still turn to executive recruiters in their searches. Here are five tips on working with recruiters, from the Cleveland-based Management Recruiters International (*www.mri.com*):

1. *Be professional.* Work with a recruiter as if that person were your colleague, coach, or client.

2. *Be honest.* Explain the extent of your job-search efforts and results. Don't conceal anything from the recruiter.

3. *Be forthright.* Explicitly share with your recruiter what you are willing to do for your next job—as well as what you are not—*especially* regarding salary or relocation. Don't hesitate to give feedback after interviews are completed to let the recruiter know if you are still interested in the job.

4. *Be committed.* Follow up on what you promise to do. A lack of commitment will discourage recruiters from working with you.

5. *Be proactive.* Research recruiters in your industry even before you start actively looking for a job. That way, you'll already have the contacts you need when you want to begin a job search.

Career-Oriented Portals and Search Engines

Start with the major search engines if you have not yet narrowed in on a list of companies on your wish list: Google, Yahoo, Infoseek, HotBot, Alta Vista, Lycos, LookSmart, Dogpile, Metacrawler, and any others that may be in operation by the time you read this. Each offers job-search services of varying kinds and quality. Most of these portals also catalog URLs offering career assistance and advice, resume posting and marketing services, city and state resource centers, employment ads in publications, executive recruiters, and a variety of job databases worldwide. One of the more comprehensive of these portals is Google. Let's walk through the options at this site to see what we might learn:

1. On Google's home page (*www.google.com*), click "Business" under the "Directory" heading.

2. This leads to the option of choosing "Employment," and under that, "Job search." Here, you will be offered 10 possible avenues, among them executive search, industries, interview advice, recruiters, resume advice, and

worldwide. On the same page are links to 100 or so job-search companies. Let's click the "By Industry" option.

3.　At this option, you can choose among 12 industry sources, as well as 50 company Websites (on the day we looked). Google is one big directory, at every level and category, providing no data of its own, but rather providing a repository of the top companies specializing in any given category.

4.　Here, you'll also find five research tools (salaries, companies, industries, occupations, and relocations). You'll also find a Browse Jobs option. (Let's say your specialty is information technology. You'll find numerous IT positions under such subcategories as engineering; information technology; and media, arts, and design.) There are also profiles of leading companies headquartered in that city. The "companies" option under "Research Tools," for example, features in-depth company profiles of more than 1,000 companies, through a link to *www.WetFeet.com*. Relocation, a little farther down, allows you to compare U.S. cities by cost of living, real estate, and quality of life, among other things.

Newsgroups

Sreenath Sreenivasan, an associate professor who teaches advanced Web reporting and writing at the Columbia University Graduate School of Journalism, recommends newsgroups as an underutilized research source. Deja (*www.deja.com/usenet*), for example, contains 35,000 newsgroups discussing everything—from aliens to Zen. It is likely that there are one or more newsgroups under your function or industry. Most of the newsgroups have archives, where you'll find even more specialized groups. Just poke around until you find what you want.

Sreenivasan suggests using a "walk-away" e-mail address available from a free e-mail company such as Juno or Hotmail, just to keep your life simple. To get his monthly e-mail message with tips about new and useful sites, write him at *sreetips@sree.net*. Sreenivasan's Website (*www.sree.net*) provides more valuable links. (You can also schedule one of his Web surfing classes there.)

Networking and Information Interviewing

Networking

More people are hired through networking than in any other way, by an overwhelming factor. Put simply, networking improves your chances of finding a job in direct proportion to the number of people you meet in your function, specialty, and industry. Be shameless. Use your family, friends, colleagues, school, church, and community acquaintances to get the word out. Here are few other underused resources:

- Call customers, clients, and suppliers with whom you developed good relationships.
- Attend class reunions, and trade fairs and conventions in your field.
- Keep a supply of business cards and resumes available at all times.
- Master a 30-second description of your background and accomplishments that you can transmit to anyone in a position to help you.

From the employer's point of view, finding a good person cost-free is an attractive alternative to a lengthy search. Saving the price of recruitment fees, advertising, and human resources department hours—all allocated to the hiring process—gives qualified candidates an added advantage in the eyes of the hiring authority. You've heard of the hidden job market? This—together with the information interviews described in the following section—is the rock you'll find it under. (See Exercise 12 on page 111 for advice on setting up your network.)

To take networking to the next level, investigate ExecuNet (www.execunet.com). Founded in 1988 and online since 1995, ExecuNet is the first and most successful online career site for more than $100,000 executives. Through introductions to recruiters or prospective employers—either online or in person at one or more of its dozens of monthly networking events in the U.S. and Canada—more than 100,000 member-executives have found new positions, built new management teams, or otherwise advanced their careers. Job-search tips are posted online weekly, and a quarterly newsletter keeps members informed about a variety of career-related topics.

Information Interviews

The progress you make networking can be consolidated by meeting one-on-one with the best decision makers you meet in group settings who work in your function or industry. Networking is an ideal forum for generating information interviews with individuals willing to describe the inner workings of a company that interests you. It can provide insight to respective advantages and disadvantages for the slight change of career you've been considering.

To set up an information interview, don't even suggest that you're looking for a job—just information. (And this should be *the truth*.) Make your meeting an information *exchange*, offering what you know about situations your interviewer may ask you about. By doing so, you've just added a valuable networking contact. She has helped you; maybe you can return the favor down the road. In addition, always ask your new contact for the names of individuals who would expand your network exponentially. If you can use her name—or if she is willing to make a call or send an e-mail of introduction—you have maximized the value of the information interview.

To get the most value from your time spent, prepare questions beforehand centering on your interviewer's background. Use the sources that got you interested in the first place: a magazine or newspaper article, a Website you discovered after a search, or the friend of a friend.

Let's say you're a mechanical engineer talking with a CEO who runs a small start-up dedicated to collecting renewable energy from the wind or the sun. Find out what got her started and what drives her to succeed. In the early part of the interview, turn all questions about yourself back to the interviewer after a short, polite response. You're there to learn. The only way to do it is to ask questions, absorb the answers, and attempt to match them with your long-range goals.

Take note of every nugget of information that touches on your interests and objectives. When you've gotten as much of the story as you need, begin to frame questions that will illuminate intersections between your background and skill sets and the interviewer's objectives, organization, and possible problems—that you might help solve.

After every information interview, write a note of thanks. If you think a possibility exists for a match, add a few paragraphs sketching out a solution to a problem that came up during the conversation or perhaps an idea for improving a technique that occurred to you on the drive home.

Tip: It may happen in the course of your job-search multitasking that you come across phone numbers or e-mail addresses you can't match with people or companies. No problem. Several reverse search engines will provide a name after you plug in the number or address. Try AT&T's Websites *www.anywho.com* or *www.whitepages.com*, or *www.reversedirectory.net*. Just remember that only listed phone numbers are accessible.

I offer one current case study to demonstrate the power of the information interview:

Ron (we'll call him), a client with whom I am working, is a recently downsized sales manager in the semiconductor field. About a month after his exit interview, he was on a trip with his long-distance cycling group. He learned that an acquaintance who occasionally rode with his group was the semi-retired general counsel for a local medical software corporation. On the company Website, Ron discovered even more: A director of operations opening had been posted for one of the firm's divisions. This was a bit of a stretch for him—and was outside his industry—but the opportunity was attractive. And from the way the job was described, he thought he might have a real shot. The general counsel gave Ron the name of the EVP to whom the division president reported. On the strength of the good word put in by counsel, Ron was able to arrange an information interview.

The meeting went well, and led to the EVP's scheduling meetings with not one, but two division presidents. Ron's next task was to neutralize his industry ignorance, as well as research all aspects of the director of operations requisition. He matched his previous accomplishments and duties with those delineated in the job description. By making a few phone calls, he was able to identify a friend of an acquaintance—a programmer in that division. She provided valuable information about the way things worked in the division, including a few observations about the president's managerial style (freewheeling, decisive, intuitive). Ron believed that one key question regarding the opening was to find out why it had been on the job board for three months.

The following week, Ron met with both division presidents, where his preliminary conclusions were confirmed: The director of operations position was the most promising opening currently available, and he had gotten along extremely well with the president. In asking about the length of time the job had been open, Ron found out that the president had been trying to perform operations duties as well as his own. Ron found out what the challenges were, and was able to indicate similar problems he had dealt with in his previous two jobs.

(The first meeting also had gone well, but there were no opportunities available in the foreseeable future.)

After the meeting Ron wrote the following e-mail message to the EVP:

> Alex,
>
> Just a quick update. I met with Rudy Jacobs last week and Jim Finley today. Both meetings went very well. The Director of Operations position in Jim's System Division sounds especially interesting. I am looking forward to further discussions with Jim on this topic.
>
> I really appreciate your assistance in making these meetings happen. I will keep you informed as things develop.
>
> Regards,
>
> Ron

Later that day, Ron received the following reply: "Good luck. Sounds like a good fit." Ron's strategy was to keep the EVP in the loop, knowing that the two division presidents would report back to him regarding the "courtesy interviews" they had conducted. By the EVP's acknowledgment of the interview, he was able to convey that Ron was still very much in the running for the job he wanted. His tactical decision was to wait to contact both division presidents until he had his second meeting with Jim Finley.

There is no assurance that Ron will get the director of operations job. On the other hand, he is now confident that he knows how to capitalize on a networking opportunity, and convert an information interview into a job interview. There was luck involved in his chance meeting with the semi-retired corporate counsel. But Ron took full advantage of that break. He is now able to treat his information interviews like sales calls, and has become more and more confident as the process has evolved. He's gotten extremely skilled at his current job of finding a job. And soon, he's convinced, he'll be able to quit.

Relocation Research

If your target companies are in locations requiring a move, find out all you can about comparative costs and salaries in your new destination. Factor in all increased expenses

Slumping Economy Hits Recruiters Hard

Small recruiters sprang up by the thousands during the booming 1990s. Now, with the job market weakening, they are taking it on the chin. Hundreds have gone out of business in recent months, and more are on the brink.

Robert Higbee, president of Higbee Associates, a Rowayton, Connecticut search firm, is working out of his dining room after giving up his $4,000-a-month office space this year. Most of his business placing management consultants has vanished, he says. His four staffers are at their homes most of the time, staying in touch by e-mail. Two other recruiters were laid off in March 2001 after a brutal stretch, during which seven search assignments were canceled in one month.

Mr. Higbee also started pitching software to job seekers last fall and welcomes the added revenue. His $40 downloadable product, titled YourJobSearcher, scours career sites for jobs. The firm, which used to count General Electric Capital Corp. as a client, also now seeks recruiting work from nonprofits and smaller firms without an HR department. "We'll look at anything now that makes sense," Mr. Higbee said.

—Kris Maher
The Wall Street Journal

(such as housing costs) as negotiating points when time comes to talk compensation (see Chapter 7). Websites including such information are: *www.homefair.com*, *www.infoplease.com*, *www.bestplaces.net*, and *www.salary.com*.

Submitting Your Resume Online

As an easy-to-use option, consider the Portable Document Format (PDF) to transmit your resume to prospective employers. PDF is a universal file format that preserves the fonts and formatting of the source document, regardless of software application. The primary benefit of the PDF format is that the document is "embedded," rather than browser dependent, and so will look the same regardless of browser. Converting a document to PDF format requires Adobe Acrobat software, which may be purchased at a number of online sources, or leased from Adobe by the month or year. PDF Viewer, on the other hand, is free and available on the Adobe Website: *www.adobe.com*.

When you've internalized all of the arcane electronic rules you used to prepare your electronic resume (see Chapter 4), which online-friendly version do you use? Sheila

Brackenbury, a Vermont Website developer, has this to say:

> I always prepare ASCII resumes with the scanner in mind. Often, those companies that ask for an ASCII version will scan it anyway, so this way you can write one version to fit both kinds of situations. Some of the firms we've dealt with online will say, "Send us your ASCII and attach your Word (or WordPerfect) document." So you send them the plain one; they'll quickly scan through it for keywords or whatever, and then they've got the nice Word doc to keep on file.
>
> Most of the bigger job-posting sites—MonsterBoard and HotJobs, and others, I'm sure—will walk you through the process. Some of them have online forms you can fill out. At the JobBank in Vermont, job seekers write resumes from the print versions they have in front of them. So you don't post an ASCII document, you write it online.

Many of the newer Internet companies seem not to be as good about acknowledging receipt of resumes as the brick-and-mortar people. It may be that inquiries received by computer rather than by mail contribute to a dehumanization of the process, where a signed letter somehow makes the candidate seem more "real."

Checking What the Employer Will See

Before sending off your first electronic resume, e-mail it and your cover letter to yourself. This test will enable you to fix all the glitches and not risk rejection from an employer before you get a chance to discuss the job itself.

Exercise 12
Setting Up Your Network

"It's not what you know, it's who you know." To both test this cliché and set up your network, answer the following questions:

Who do you know who is employed by a company you might want to work for—or one of its competitors?

_____

_____

_____

_____

_____

Who do you know who does the kind of work you want to be hired to do?

_____

_____

_____

_____

_____

_____

_____

_____

Who do you know who seems to be well-connected?

_____

_____

_____

_____

_____

_____

_____

_____

_____

Who do you know (even slightly) from professional or trade associations?

_____

_____

_____

_____

_____

_____

_____

Who do you know from your last job who would be willing to put you in touch with others?

_____

_____

_____

_____

_____

_____

_____

Who else did you come into contact with in your last job who might have leads (for example, suppliers or customers)?

_____

_____

_____

_____

_____

_____

_____

Who do you know from school or alumni associations who might have contacts or be good contacts themselves?

_____

_____

_____

_____

_____

_____

_____

Who in your extended family might be of help?

_____

_____

_____

_____

_____

_____

The idea in networking is to get those you contact initially to refer you to others.

●●●

Whether you come up with five names or 50, the number of your contacts will grow as you ask each person you approach for the names of two or three others you might talk to. A contact interview, whether in person or on the phone, should be viewed as an opportunity to promote your skills and accomplishments.

Most people are flattered when you ask their advice, and most people get satisfaction from helping others. There's no reason to feel uncomfortable about setting up your network and using it.

Chapter 6

Interviewing to Communicate and Convince

"Whenever two people meet, there are really six people present.
There is each man as he sees himself,
each man as the other person sees him,
and each man as he really is."

—William James

S tripped to its essence, a job interview is a business meeting, nothing more or less. The "buyer," better known as the prospective employer, has real needs to fill. The "seller," or job seeker, has the potential to fill those needs. From the point of view of the job seeker, the success of the interview depends solely on an ability to demonstrate—or "sell"—this need.

A New Generation of Interviewers

Our nation's soft economy over the past several years, coupled with a proliferation of corporate failures has led to an unprecedented number of unemployed workers. One unfortunate fallout is that an ever-growing talent pool of men and women is available for interviews—some of them for positions you seek as well. For this reason the job-search challenge is becoming increasingly complex for everyone looking for a better job.

Connecticut's Pratt & Whitney, a division of United Technologies, is one of many larger corporations to have devised a systematized, sophisticated hiring process for evaluating managerial candidates. A team leader (usually the hiring executive) explains the process to the other team members. All first-time interviewers attend a one-on-one planning session with a lead interviewer, and sit in on live interviews before conducting one of their own. The group decides which aspects of the interview will be handled by each member.

Each candidate is evaluated in six general categories according to a number of criteria, among them:

- *Achievement*: Attains established objectives on schedule and demonstrates follow-through and persistence despite obstacles.
- *Managing change*: Develops and implements decisions that respond to or bring about change; executes timely, logical decisions; takes calculated risks.
- *Leading by example*: Adheres to business and personal principles and performance standards; develops trust and exhibits leadership across normal functional boundaries.
- *Creating a shared vision*: Perceives business issues and their integration into a vision and communicates this vision to the organization.
- *Building constructive relationships*: Demonstrates sound judgment in staff selection, assignment, and delegation; shows respect for others; communicates effectively.
- *Technical competence*: Acquires, processes, and applies knowledge to appropriate business opportunities and problems.

United Technologies employs a rigorous executive selection process evaluating 18 "key success characteristics" in five categories (see Table 1). Interviewers use at least two success characteristics for each category in every candidate assessment, a minimum of 10 characteristics per candidate. Not all companies use such a systematic matrix, of course, but some of them do. It will be worth your while to speak with a current or former executive at your target companies to get some idea of the interview procedures and rationale in place.

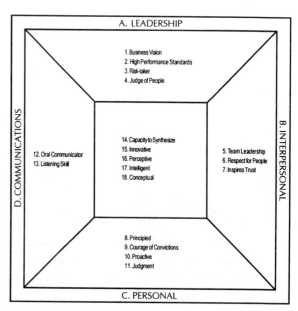

Table 1. Key Success Characteristics for United Technologies Executives

Do Your Homework

The key to generating interviews that lead to job offers is preparation. The more knowledgeable you are about the position, the company, and the industry, the easier it will be for you to demonstrate your ability to solve a company's problems, generate new business, or help save it money. Only then can your prospective boss visualize you on the payroll.

Sound interview preparation makes good sense for three reasons:

1. *The more you know about a company and the way it works, the easier it is to project yourself as a permanent, full-time employee.* Learning about a company's strengths, weaknesses, and problem areas, from customers, vendors, and competitors, as well as from current and former employees, adds texture and objectivity not included in information supplied by the company itself. Being able to converse knowledgeably about a company's strengths and weaknesses allows a candidate to be viewed as a professional who thoroughly investigates a situation before acting upon it. This, in turn, allows a prospective employer to more easily visualize the candidate's ability to perform his duties in a consistently effective manner.

2. *The more a person knows about a company, the more likely it will be that he is perceived as a problem-solver.* Speaking lucidly about new product lines, a current advertising campaign, or recent public statements by company officers permits a candidate to use up-to-date data that leads to greater rapport with a prospective employer, along with a better opportunity to deepen the relationship.

3. *The more a person knows about a company, the easier it will be to decide whether he wants to work there.* Learning the finer distinctions about relationships among departments and divisions, along with the respective managers and staff, helps to recognize the value a company places on performance. In turn, it shows how it rewards employees for exemplary performance.

Interviewing Outside an Industry or Function

If you are changing careers from your current industry or function, however slight it is, planning and positioning become even more important. A similar burden falls on the repackaging of such written credentials as your resumes and cover letters (see Chapter 4). You have passed the first test in the process simply by generating the interview in the first place. But because you will be viewed by some interviewers as an industry or functional alien, your qualifications may be called into question in ways that may surprise you. For this reason, it is important that you speak with some knowledge about your target company's customers, competitors, and clients, as well as its infrastructure. Extensive information interviews with representatives of your new industry or function are a must.

Due Diligence

Whether your interview was set up by a search firm, the result of your answering an ad, or was generated by one of your networks, the first part of your preparation should be focused on the company itself. Here are some questions you need to answer:

- What specific position is the company looking to fill?
- What attracted you to this job?
- Reading between the lines, what are some of the intangible needs the company wants to fill?
- What skills are needed for the job? (For each skill you identify, think of specific examples of situations in which you have demonstrated that skill.)
- What were the company's revenues and profits last year and the year before?
- What is the company's market share vis-à-vis its competitors?
- What problems (or challenges, or opportunities) is the company facing?
- Why do these problems exist?
- How might they be overcome?

Next, investigate the available position and your prospective boss. The information you need won't appear in an ad. If you are working with an executive recruiter, be sure to ask your counselor the following questions. If you are on your own, use one or more of the previously mentioned sources to get as much information as you can.

- Why is the position open?
- When was it last open, and why?
- How long has it been open? (If two months or more, why is it so tough to fill?)
- Where is the person who previously held the job? Can you talk with him?
- How many people have been interviewed so far?
- How many candidates are in the running? Why are they still being considered?
- What are the prospects for advancement?
- What will be the determining factor in getting the job?
- How many others in the company are doing the same work?

- How will performance be measured?
- Who is the boss? What is her title?
- How long has she been with the company?
- What is her management style?
- What are her prospects with the company?

Preliminary Telephone Interviews

Frequently a company will screen marginal candidates to assure that only the most qualified are brought in for face-to-face interviews. The most convenient way to do this is to spend time on the phone. From the interviewer's point of view it minimizes the possibility that a good candidate will be overlooked. But it also enables you as interviewee to ask qualifying questions that will help measure your continued interest in the job.

If you are asked to talk by phone with your prospective boss or a senior representative from human resources, your single objective is to make a positive enough impression during your phone interview to upgrade your candidacy to the next level. In addition to taking time to research the company, here are the four steps crucial to generating an in-person interview:

1. *Ask for a specific definition of the ideal candidate.* If you know what qualities the company considers most important, all of your subsequent questions—and your answers to the interviewer's questions—can be framed with this awareness in mind.

2. *Project yourself as that candidate.* Without knowing what the accomplishments, skills, and job experience most crucial to doing the best job are, as determined by company officers, you have no idea which aspects of your rich experience to emphasize. A war story you are most proud of may have no bearing on the job to be done, and may be a waste of the interviewer's time. Getting a firsthand definition of the qualifications key to peak performance allows you to emphasize only those aspects of your professional background relevant to the opening.

3. *Find out what top two or three challenges need to be faced first.* This defines you as a proactive candidate, anxious to take on the toughest aspects of the job.

4. *Demonstrate your ability and willingness to face these challenges.* Every employer wants to hire problem-solvers. Taking the initiative in learning what problems exist—and perhaps asking if one or more of the solutions that occur to you have yet been considered—puts you in that category.

Your sole objective in the telephone interview is to generate a face-to-face invitation. This being true, it is not in your best interest at this stage to:

- Ask about salary or benefits.
- Ask about possible company problems.
- Ask potentially negative questions about the corporate culture.

None of these questions will enhance your prospects of an invitation to corporate headquarters to meet your prospective colleagues. Some could even hurt your chances. Keep this conversation moving forward, putting yourself—and your candidacy—in the most positive possible light.

The 4 Parts of a Job Interview

If your telephone interview goes well, the next step will be to visit the employer's office(s), or a mutually agreed upon site if interviews have been arranged for several candidates in the same geographical area.

The following breakdown of a job interview is written from your point of view as the interviewee, and includes most of the elements that helped make your telephone interview go smoothly. No interview will unfold the way you think it will, simply because you are a guest on the interviewer's turf. By definition, you are not in control, and most attempts on your part to gain control likely will fail. Consequently, you need to keep firmly in mind the points you must emphasize to make the best possible case for a job offer. If you are well prepared, you can do this without affecting the rhythm of the interviewer's agenda—and still inject points and get answers to key questions that are crucial to your candidacy. If you are working with a skilled interviewer, this will not be a problem. She wants to hire the best candidate as badly as you want to be perceived as that candidate.

According to the videotape *Interview to Win* (Wilson McLeran, Inc., © 2000), the four key things to be accomplished in a job interview are:

1. Make the best first impression.
2. Get a definition of the ideal candidate.
3. Make sure you want the job.
4. Work to get a job offer, or at least a second interview. (A fifth topic covered in the video, "negotiating compensation," is dealt with in Chapter 7.)

The Best First Impression

There is no question that a bad first impression can kill your chances for a job, even in a preliminary screening interview. No matter how impressive your qualifications, an interviewer can decide almost immediately that you just won't do. This judgment may have nothing to do with your ability to handle the job, and thus be completely beyond your control. Here are some of the reasons for being knocked out of contention:

Physical Appearance

To use a military metaphor, let's say a sergeant needs six "volunteers" for morning latrine and kitchen duty. The recruits who routinely escape such assignments are those who rely on a knack for virtual invisibility while in formation. They're clean shaven, have shined shoes, and don't qualify for additional judgmental scrutiny. Those more easily identified—with wrinkled shirts, dull brass, cockeyed caps, or whatever—are usually available in sufficient quantity to fill out any duty roster.

What's the point? Don't draw attention to yourself in any way that distracts the interviewer from your message and objective.

For the most part, passing the interview physical appearance test is largely a matter of exercising common sense. Those found wanting in any aspect of this relatively superficial, often subtle, but nevertheless seriously considered criterion will be assumed deficient in other respects as well, and almost certainly will be passed over. Here are three commonly abused areas:

1. *Basic business dress.* Part of the definition of common sense as it applies to this relatively mundane-sounding point has to do with knowing where you are. Make it your business to know, particularly if you are moving to a different part of the country, what "appropriate" dress means. A corporate opening in New York, Los Angeles, or Chicago, for example, whether for a department head or a chief financial officer, may mean adhering to a higher level of formality, sophistication, or awareness of style than would apply in less fashion-conscious parts of the country.

    If your taste in clothes is marginal or worse, ask someone with good fashion sense to help put together one or two interview outfits. Be prepared to make a sizable investment, and avoid polyester shortcuts that may save bucks but lose you the job offer. The thing is, you want nothing so superficial as a jangling earring or a loud tie to dilute your ultimate message: You can do the job well, and you can manage your future team effectively.

2. *Neatness.* Sure it counts—more with some prospective employers than with others, but either way don't allow a hiring decision to rest on such a frivolous lack of attention to detail.

    These are all obvious considerations anyway: shined shoes, clean and pressed clothes, combed hair, close shave, clean nails. Get to your destination five minutes early, in order to allow time for a restroom check that will correct windblown hair or a lettuce-covered tooth.

3. *Hygiene.* This may sound all too obvious, but leave nothing to chance; take time enough to shower in the morning rather than the night before. Use whatever deodorant/antiperspirant that will keep you both dry and relatively odorless. Use mouthwash if bad breath has been a problem. If you have a cold not severe enough to postpone your meeting, take whatever medication will control coughing or sneezing.

Body Language and Mannerisms

Too much probably has been made of the impact involuntary movements and gestures have on an interviewer and what they disclose about a candidate's motives and possible hidden agenda. Entire books are devoted to their variations and subtleties. Even so, what you do with your hands and face during the interview—even inadvertently—can sometimes be misinterpreted as an indication or possible absence of candor.

If you are trying to hide part of your past and think you can fool your interviewer—either by omission or commission—just remember that she may have ways of countering your deception.

Dennis M. Kowal, a U.S. Army Intelligence psychologist, wrote in the human resources magazine *Personnel Journal* that 80 percent of communication is nonverbal, and that 80 percent of *that* communication reveals itself in a person's face, particularly in the eyes. He counsels interviewers to recognize the subtle, nonverbal clues that indicate an attempt to deceive. Few applicants can lie without feeling a tightness in the stomach, which usually is manifest by an involuntary change in facial expression and a decrease of eye contact with the interviewer.

Sometimes nonverbal and verbal cues are combined. For example, a person will use an expression like "To tell the truth" or "To be perfectly honest," accompanied by a major break in eye contact, a shift in body orientation, or a movement of hand to face that results in an obvious physical contradiction.

Dishonesty has no place in the interview, obviously, and will probably be uncovered sooner or later anyway. The point is that because more and more interviewers are trained to recognize it, dishonesty becomes not only wrong but stupid.

Mannerisms

Many people aren't aware of facial tics or idiosyncratic mannerisms that may stand in the way of their making a positive first impression. If you have a doubt in this regard, ask at least two friends or close family members to identify any possible physical distractions that may negatively affect your interviewing first impression. You may have a correctable physical, psychological, or neurological problem; but you won't be able to fix it until you have it diagnosed.

Other Causes of Fear and Discomfort

Most other reasons for feeling that one would rather be anywhere but in an interview usually are grounded in a lack of preparation—either in the interview or the job itself. This leads to a rapid drop in confidence, which in turn reveals itself in telltale body language.

After learning as much as you can about the job, the company, and the interviewer, examine your credentials. Be ready to defend your ability to handle any of the prospective responsibilities, including those you find out about for the first time in the interview.

Be able as well to identify and neutralize any possible weaknesses for the position you think you may have. Anticipating the worst and knowing how you will deal with it will lead to a peace of mind (or at least a reduction of panic).

Vocabulary and Diction

Some of you may argue that your job doesn't require sophisticated communication skills, which will sharply reduce any significance you might give to mastering the English language. The thing is, every job interviewee needs sufficient self-expression skills to get the job offer in the first place.

If a weakness in vocabulary or grammar is a problem of yours, remedy it at all costs. Minor gaps in your knowledge can be taken care of with assiduous study of a good, compact text, such as Strunk and White's *The Elements of Style* (see the Bibliography at the end of the book), as well as numerous vocabulary improvement programs available in book and audio tape format. More serious problems will require formal study at a local community college or adult education center. Consult your telephone directory for a good institution nearby.

If you're unsure as to how serious your problem is, ask to take a test at one of the two local sources mentioned above. On a day-to-day basis, carry a pocket dictionary with you or write down every word whose pronunciation or meaning you are unsure of, as a reminder to look them up at the end of the day.

Problems of New Citizens

Those of you for whom English is a second (or third) language face a more difficult problem. Not only will you have to demonstrate your facility for mastering a new tongue, with all of its implied nuances, but you must be perceived as acculturated enough to adapt quickly to your new supervisors, peers, and subordinates, as well as to comport yourself appropriately in any professionally generated exposure to the media. (See "Are You Ready for Your Close-Up?" on page 147.) You may need to hire a coach, or make a friend of someone in the industry you have identified, to familiarize yourself with professional colloquialisms, buzzwords, and vocabulary. This is tricky, of course, because "in" words and phrases have a way of going "out" overnight. You'll be judged more harshly for using dated expressions and references than for staying with the tried, the true, and the generic.

Sometimes a candidate's accent or dialectic pattern calls attention to itself and distracts from the message. Minor problems can be corrected through numerous available audiotape programs. Individuals with accents so pronounced that understandability is a problem may need to consult a speech pathologist trained in accent reduction (Yes, that's what they call it.) For names of local specialists, check your telephone directory, a hospital or clinic, or a nearby university speech department.

Preparedness

One area of preparation that may affect a good first impression is embodied in a question that certainly will be asked early in the interview if your resume dates reveal either an employment gap, or an end date in the "current" employment entry on your resume.

Here's the question: "I see that you left Carstairs Industries in July. What was the situation there, by the way?"

If you have lost a job recently, you need to be able to answer this question, or any of its many variations, in a way that satisfies your interviewer that your past will not adversely affect your future with their company. (Job loss was covered thoroughly in Chapter 1.) We visit this topic again here because if it is brought up early enough in an interview, it could mean a make-or-break first impression.

Write your own scenario in preparing to deal with your particular situation, making sure to cover the following points:

1. *Don't knock your former employer.* Many victims of job loss blame individuals at the company they left for their troubles. This is especially true of very recent terminees, who sometimes spend so much time grieving about their lost job that they render themselves impotent in their search for a new one. Pursuing this path invariably stamps you, accurately or not, as a vindictive whiner unable to put the past behind you. This is not a demeanor conducive to job offers.

2. *Don't dwell on negatives.* Wallowing in the misfortune of your most recent job experience similarly conveys the message that your past supersedes the present in terms of your priorities. No meaningful search for employment can move forward until you expel the residue from a bad previous job.

3. *Accept responsibility you deserve.* Look within yourself for the maturity and introspection to examine your last employment situation objectively. List and acknowledge the pivotal mistakes you made and how much they

may have contributed to the loss of your job. This level of detachment may require some help from one or more of your former colleagues. Ask for brutal honesty, to be sure you are not protecting yourself from responsibility you rightfully deserve (see Chapter 2). Then be certain you can handle the honesty, in case it contradicts your still subjective recollections.

4.   *Identify positive outcomes.* Marshaling your total efforts for a job search can be effective only after you reach closure from your previous job. Analyze the reasons for your mistakes and establish a game plan for translating them into learning experiences you can take to your next job and profit from.

Your story may bear no resemblance to the following scripted example (taken from the video *Interview to Win* referenced on page 120). However, the four principles described above should be adhered to without exception.

Interviewer: I see that you left Carstairs Industries in July. How did that come about?

Candidate: Actually, I was dismissed.

Interviewer: Oh? What was the situation there?

Candidate: Well, it seemed that my boss and I had very different workways. He replaced the previous group vice president who had hired me.

Interviewer: What do you mean, the two of you had "very different workways"?

Candidate: Well, he wanted a lot more frequent feedback than I was used to providing. With my previous boss, I was in the habit of just doing the best job I could on my own, after I was clear about the department's objectives. My new boss had other expectations. He wanted to be briefed on a daily basis. This was a constant tension between us.

Interviewer: What happened, specifically?

Candidate: I had seen a few of the danger signs a couple of months earlier, but obviously I didn't do enough about them to change the situation. Actually, things had been getting worse for about six months, and then bingo—I was gone.

Interviewer: How do you view the experience with the hindsight you have now?

Candidate: It was a fundamental learning experience, I can tell you that. Maybe I was a little bit arrogant. I don't know. I certainly was shortsighted. Underneath it all, I probably was taking out my resentment on my new boss. I really liked the guy who had hired me, and I thought he had been treated unfairly. Bottom line is, I know what went wrong and I know it won't happen again. The experience has taught me to be a much better communicator. Would you like any more detail than this?

Interviewer: No, thank you. I appreciate your frank response.

Don't rely on a memorized, word-for-word presentation to get you through this interview land mine. First of all, unless you are a superb actor your response will *sound* memorized—and by definition be suspect. Instead, prepare answers (in substance, not word for word) to as many questions as you can think of related to the reason(s) you lost your job.

Your answers will vary, of course, with the situation. Not only that, different interviewers will ask for differing amounts of detail, depending on their perspective. For this reason, your answers should be structured on a "need to know" basis: most relevant information first, with less important details following, and *only* if the interviewer asks for them. Structure all of your answers with the four principles of overcoming a job loss objection just discussed firmly in mind. Here are a few related questions you may face:

- Why do you think things got as bad as they did?
- What do you think you could have done to change things that you didn't do?
- To what extent was your job performance an issue, do you think?
- Why weren't you able to get along with your boss (or with whomever else there may have been a problem)?
- Couldn't you see this coming?
- Why did it take you so long to get a handle on the situation?
- When you saw that your job was in jeopardy, why didn't you go to your boss about it? (If your relationship with your boss *was* the problem: "Would it have been politically possible for you to go to your boss's boss?" or "Wasn't there a colleague you could have asked to intercede on your behalf?")
- Have you had similar problems on other jobs?
- Now that you have this experience behind you, what would you have done differently?

The key is to be so well prepared that you can answer all questions calmly and assertively—meanwhile keeping in mind the four principles of neutralizing your job loss described earlier.

Poor Listening Skills

Far and away the most important interviewing skill to master is listening. It is especially important to listen carefully during the first minutes because your answers to the initial questions will set the tone for the rest of the meeting and determine the lasting impression you create.

The key to effective listening is concentration. Steel yourself to focus single-mindedly on the questions you are being asked, the way they are being asked, and any subtleties or hidden meanings that may lurk within them. Here are the most common examples of this attention lapse and how to prevent them.

Inattentiveness

Often a candidate's concentration will waver before the interviewer has finished the question, and in so doing, part of its meaning will be lost. Stay with the question until it is complete. Then frame your answer.

Missing Nuances

A friendly smile may mask a question behind a question, which you won't catch if your antennae are not up all the way. A frequently asked opening question like: "Tell me about yourself," or one of its variations, sounds harmless enough. You'll lose points, though, if your response is rambling, halting, scattered, overlong, or too detailed; is infused with personal rather than professional history; or excessively repeats your resume entries.

Your questioner wants to know what is important to you. Because the question is open-ended, you can answer it any way you want. Rehearse (but don't let it appear to sound so) a 15- or 20-second answer that is bare bones and hits the highlights of your professional career that best matches the description of the *job you are interviewing for*, insofar as you know it. Skip childhood, college, marriage, and children. Cut right to your growth record in the industry or your function, whichever is the more powerful story. (The interviewer probably has not only read your resume thoroughly, but has it in front of her as you speak.) "Tell me about yourself" is an opportunity for some creative packaging and one of the few interview opportunities you will have for control.

Hearing What You Want to Hear

Not being completely prepared for your interview can cause your attention to wander while your interviewer asks her questions. This may happen if you want a job very badly and are overeager to make a good impression. If the reason for your overeagerness is that you are out of work and are desperate for a paycheck, you must sublimate your panic attack at all costs. Your state of mind will be obvious to your interviewer, and your chances of continuing as a viable candidate will be reduced sharply.

Recruiter Geologists

"There are three people on our recruitment team I call "Internet geologists." They go through some tough training, but they're able to search strings, to really drill down into Websites: They'll flip sites, x-ray them all the way down to the personal Web pages. (It's not uncommon for many of the technical people to show off a bit and put their resume on their personal pages.)

"But these aren't the people we're after. The ones with resumes are trolling. We're looking for candidates who aren't looking for us. We just interviewed 12 people for sales positions. The two we liked were the only ones who had not posted resumes. We asked what their most desirable position would be if they were to make a change. We found out their horsepower was not being tapped directly and were able to give them what they didn't have."

—K.C. Donovan, VP, Human Resources
Globix Corporation

Active Listening

Arthur Bell and Dayle Smith, on pages 35-36 of their book *Winning With Difficult People* (Barron's Educational Series, Inc., 1991), talk about "active listening" as an alternative to anger when dealing with difficult people. Much of what they say is applicable to the hiring interview situation, from first impressions to later stages of the interview. Bell and Smith describe two techniques to help put active listening into play. I've adapted them slightly for our purposes here:

- *Technique 1:* At the outset, consciously turn off all prejudgments and assumptions about the interview. "Let it happen" in the same way a movie unfolds before you. Try to ask more questions than you usually do ("What do you mean?" "Tell me more about that." "Can you give me an example?")
- *Technique 2:* Repeat some of the interviewer's key phrases to help clarify points you don't completely understand. Be sure your tone is one of interest, not judgment.

Interviewer: A large part of the first several months, then, would be spent in fieldwork.

Candidate: Fieldwork...

Interviewer: Yes, fieldwork. Getting out into the territories to find out what the dealers are thinking...what their problems are....This is what it will take to get this new product airborne.

Repeating words or phrases—in moderation, to be sure—can be an effective alternative to the clarification questions asked in Technique 1. Still, the key word in the phrase "active listening" is "listening." Without your antennae out there, concentrating 100 percent for the duration of the interview, any additional tactics are rendered meaningless.

Get a Definition of the Ideal Candidate

Presenting yourself as the candidate best able to do the job presupposes a thorough knowledge of the job itself—or as many aspects of it as you can learn before and during the interview. This breaks down into two parts: Defining the job and identifying your target company's problems.

Defining the Job

Without a comprehensive knowledge of the job, projecting yourself as the ideal candidate will be impossible. The better interviewers, as well as interviewers at companies with well-thought-out hiring policies, will make this easy to accomplish. They know that the best way to determine which candidates are the best match for the position is to share as much nonproprietary information about the job's responsibilities and challenges as they can.

However, this is not a position universally held. In his book *On Hiring,* accounting recruiter Robert Half cautions interviewers "not to describe the job until *after* you elicit information from the candidate. [emphasis his] It's a tactical mistake in the early stages of the interview to reveal details about the position, beyond a general job description." (When experts write books for *interviewers* describing the best ways to keep candidates in the dark, your job becomes even tougher.)

Half's reasoning is that if details about the job are given away too soon, a candidate may be able to falsely tailor his background to the open job. If early in the conversation the interviewer says, for example, "We're looking for someone who is extremely well-organized and detail-minded," a shrewd candidate, according to Half, "will answer subsequent questions in a way calculated to give [the interviewer the idea] that he or she has those very qualities, whether they exist or not."

It seems unlikely that the most savvy of candidates could get away with such empty bravado, even if questioned by a marginally competent interviewer. After all, this is exactly the kind of information an interviewee must have to assure that he discusses those of his attributes closest to the employer's needs.

The point is, if you wait for the interviewer, you may not learn sufficient details about the position to present yourself as the ideal candidate. The interviewer is in the power seat, not you. Too aggressive an effort on your part to change the course of the conversation may be interpreted negatively enough to knock you out of the running.

So let's cut right to the ways you can most effectively communicate all of your job-related strengths in a way that projects you as the ideal candidate. Then test yourself to be sure you have done so. There are six good ways to stay on top of the interview and give yourself the best opportunity to become the ideal candidate:

1. Answer all questions succinctly, leaving time for your own follow-up questions.
2. Prepare your questions beforehand.
3. Ask questions that fully define the job.
4. Take notes to be sure you retain crucial information.
5. Listen for the questions behind the questions.
6. Summarize periodically to test for thoroughness and accuracy.

Identifying Potential Problems

If you don't find out what your prospective employer's problems are, there is no way for you to project yourself as the candidate best able to solve them. And the most obvious and effective way to illuminate these problems is to ask about them directly. Use any research available to you, to particularize your questions for each company at which you have scheduled interviews.

The Job:

- How long has the position been open?
- When was it last open?
- Where is the person who previously held the job?
- Why is he being replaced?

The Department:

- What are the company's long-range plans for this department?
- What is the budgeting process as it relates to this department?
- What is the department's reputation in the company?
- How is morale?

The Company:

- In my research about the company, I found that _____.
  Can you tell me anything more about this situation?
- What challenges do you think the company will face in the next year? In the next five years?
- What is the predominant management style at the company?
- Is there a definable "corporate culture"? What is it like to work here?

Determine Whether You Want the Job

There are a few ways for you to find out details about the job, the corporate culture, and the extent to which you fit the position, other than by listening to the interviewer. The first has to do with going over the previous set of "problem questions" to learn whether some trouble spots that emerge raise serious questions in your mind about the company's viability—or your viability as one of its employees. If you begin to believe that one or more company problems is likely to affect your happiness and effectiveness there, it's time to politely say goodbye.

For example, if the person you will be replacing was fired or resigned because of incompatibility with another employee who is still on the payroll, this could be a **big** red flag. You need to probe further to be sure you're not setting yourself up for the same fate.

Other problems areas that may give you pause:

- Is there too small a support staff for you to function efficiently (and an insufficient budget for outsourcing)?
- Is the company ripe for a takeover or a downsizing?
- Does the position require too much of a learning curve for you to make an immediate contribution?

Probe, probe, probe, into areas that are a concern for you, until you are completely satisfied that this is a genuine opportunity, and won't turn into a desperation paycheck. When in doubt, let your gut decide (see "Think With Your Gut," page 71).

Work to Get a Job Offer, or at Least a Second Interview

It's the interviewer's job to raise objections to your candidacy. But it's your job to overcome these objections, to the extent that you can. This starts with your resume, and the questions you will be asked about it. Treat every entry almost as a script cue. You were asked to interview because some of your skills and accomplishments matched the needs of the open position. From what you know about the opening, go over every entry

And Another Thing...

"One question I always end up asking is: 'If I were to go out on the street and talk to your peers, your ex-colleagues, and your customers, what would they say about you?' I go through this list one group at a time and invariably get useful and interesting answers."

—Paul Rand
Corporate Technology Communications

of your resume, and try to anticipate which of your qualities are most likely to have generated the company's interest in you. Think of responses to questions that will allow you to elaborate on your accomplishments.

Tough Questions

Every experienced interviewer is trained to ask questions that will expose any weaknesses in your candidacy. The best way to handle such questions is to anticipate them and be prepared for them. Write all your answers to the following questions on a sheet of paper, then memorize and practice them so you'll be ready for them when they're asked.

- What do you know about our company? (Do the research so you'll have some key information.)
- Why do you want to work for us? (Things to think about in formulating your answer: challenge, growth, potential, and experience in the field.)
- Why should we hire you? (Not because you need a job. Think about specific contributions you can make.)
- Do you object to taking a drug-screening test? (Make sure you know exactly where you stand on this. An increasing number of firms are requiring drug screening as part of their pre-employment physical.)
- If you could start again, what would you do differently? (Don't blame others for early mistakes you may have made.)
- In your present position, what problems have you identified that had previously been overlooked?

You may never have to consider the following questions and leading statements about your management style, but being prepared for them will be a useful exercise:

- Describe the approach you use to set work goals for others. Give examples of specific goals you have set for an individual or for groups.
- Describe the approach you use to set work goals for yourself. Give examples of specific goals you have set for yourself.
- Describe a situation in which a goal you set was not met: for yourself, for an individual, or for a group. How did you handle each of these situations?

Neutralize the Soft Spots

The interview is beginning to wind down when the interviewer goes into closure mode with a query, perhaps something like: "Well, do you have any questions?"

It is at this moment that you must find out where you stand. It could be your last remaining chance. If the interviewer has already made a determination to eliminate you from consideration and does not intend to share that information with you, you're dead meat. It may be a misunderstanding, or an erroneous assumption. But you almost certainly will not get a straight answer. The interviewer needs to hedge her bets. Or, she doesn't want to embarrass you by rejecting you openly. Or, she doesn't want to embarrass *herself* by transmitting a face-to-face rejection. The point is, if you've lost, you won't know it. Even worse, there's no opportunity to resurrect your candidacy. Your only hope is to take matters into your own hands.

Perhaps the way this situation was treated in the videotape *Interview to Win* will have some bearing on your own circumstances:

Interviewer: Well, I guess that about does it. Do you have any further questions?

Candidate: Yes. First of all I was wondering where you were in the hiring process. For example, have you seen everyone you're going to see?

Interviewer: No, there are three more interviews scheduled over the next week or so before we decide who to invite back a second time.

Candidate: Well, is there any way of knowing whether I will make the first cut?

Interviewer: Not really. It's a little premature at this point.

Candidate: All right. I just wanted you to know that this is a job I'm very interested in, and believe I could do well.

Interviewer: Well, this is good to know.

Candidate: Can you tell me at this point if there is anything I've said that gives you less than total confidence in my ability to do the job?

Interviewer: No, not really. You're probably not as strong in the area of long-range planning as I would like, but I don't see that as a critical factor.

Candidate: Oh, really? In that case I should mention that at Convecto, a couple of months before I was given that special project I told you about, I was asked to come up with a rationale that would either justify the project or cause us to scrap it. I put the team together that crafted the plan we finally went with.

Interviewer: Good. I'm glad you asked.

Candidate: I am, too. By the way, if there's anything else I can do to convince you I should stay in the running, I'd sure be happy to. For example, if you think of other aspects of my background you perceive to be less than ideal, let me know and I'll address them...with a trial assignment, perhaps, or anything else you think appropriate.

Interviewer: Interesting idea. Let me think about it. I may be getting back to you.

Candidate: I don't want to appear to be pushy. It's just that I know the job is right for me, and I want you to view me as a serious, capable candidate.

Interviewer: Well, that I do, believe me. Thank you for coming in.

The candidate accomplished three things in his conduct of the interview end game:

- He found out where he stood with the other candidates.
- He reaffirmed his interest in the job.
- He elevated his candidacy by every means possible.

And this is all you can do, before making preparations for the second interview.

The Second Interview

If you think you have a decent shot at becoming one of the finalists for the opening, preparation is even more important than the first time around—primarily because the competition will be stiffer. Think of the things that got you this far in the first place. Conversely, try to think of reasons you weren't offered the job at the end of the first interview.

Prepare for your second interview as follows: After reviewing your notes from the first interview, make two three-column lists. First, record all of your qualifications for the job in Column A. In Column B, list the degree to which you were able to articulate these qualifications to the interviewer. Column C will consist of the selling job that remains in the second interview—A minus B, as it were.

The second list will include specific qualifications required or desired for the position, along with any grey areas that represent all of the conceivable negatives in your candidacy. Catalog these in Column A, by category. In Column B, record the extent to which you neutralized each of these liabilities in the first interview. In Column C, detail the work that needs to be done in the second interview.

In applying these data and conclusions to the interview itself, it is essential to strike a proper balance. Overselling—either by way of reinforcing positives or eliminating negatives—can lead to an appearance of anxiety at one extreme and defensiveness at the other. Either could be a knockout factor in receiving a job offer. It is enough to be on top of the situation, determining what issues are yet a concern, and then to deal with them in a straightforward, confident manner. Depending on the circumstances, this may be an appropriate time to volunteer a trial assignment for an area in which you are perceived to be weak, but for which you have confidence in your ability.

Finally—and be careful with this suggestion, because it does involve some risk—consider seizing the opportunity and putting some distance between you and your competitors. If you're dealing with an open, pragmatic, forceful individual, see how quickly you can get to the heart of the matter in a way that will increase the regard in which you are held.

A possible interview opener for such a person might be: "Well, what can I do to convince you that I'm the best person for the job?" Or (with a slight smile), "What is preventing you from offering me the job right now?" This forcing style, mirroring as it does the personality of the interviewer, may help you to be visualized as an aggressive, contributing department member. You may well be anticipating the kind of information or attitude for which your possible boss is about to probe, to reach a judgment of her own.

Be sure you have gauged your interviewer correctly. A more reflective, controlled person would surely judge such questions to be boorish or otherwise inappropriate, enough to knock you out of the running. Such an individual will require a more subtle approach.

Chapter 7

Managing the Job Offer

> "To love what you do and feel that it matters—
> how could anything be more fun?"
>
> —Katharine Graham

Y ou've done all you can, and it's time to wait for your first job offer. Now comes your first tough decision. If the wait has been a long one, you'll be tempted to say yes immediately, even if the offer includes less than everything you have been counting on. Regardless of whether this is the first solid opportunity you've had since your severance ran out four months ago, postpone your decision until you have a chance to sort out all the positives and negatives.

Weighing the Job Offer

The way a company compensates its employees tells much about the way it values them. Competitive compensation not only attracts good people, it motivates and helps retain them. For this reason, it is in the best interests of both the employee and the employer to reach a mutually satisfactory and equitable compensation agreement.

But compensation is more than base salary. It can include equity or stock; it can include bonuses of various kinds; and it almost always will include benefits. Companies unable to offer competitive starting salaries often can make up the difference with a sign-on bonus, an improved benefits package, a performance bonus program, or a more generous relocation arrangement.

A Stock-Options Primer

- *Stock option*: The right to buy stock at a certain price at a certain time.
- *Strike price*: The price at which the option holder can buy the stock.
- *Vesting schedule*: Schedule for receiving options; most commonly spread out over three years, with one-third of the options vesting each year.
- *Exercising options*: Once you have the options, actually buying the stock at the strike price options.
- *Lockup period*: The six-month period after an initial public offering (IPO), during which company insiders cannot sell their shares.
- *Alternative minimum tax*: The tax applicable in some instances under the terms of a hefty options package.
- *"Under water"*: The unfortunate condition of having worthless options (that means, if one has the right to buy stock at $15 per share and stock falls to $10, those options are "under water").

— iVillage.com

Enlightened employers will make it a priority to accommodate the needs of exceptional candidates. Negotiating total compensation, therefore, is almost always an option.

The Employment Contract

The negotiation stage, in its raw form, involves only money—either tangibly or in the form of benefits and prequisites. Those of you at a level of roughly $100,000 annual base salary and above will want to negotiate your employment terms with a written contract or letter of agreement (this figure will vary from industry to industry, even company to company).

A small number of companies go even further. In setting up a board of advisors to help put together a compensation policy for Chicago's Corporate Technology Communications, CEO Paul Rand included both legal and accounting counsel. "We decided early on," says Rand, "that every employee would get a contract. Part of the reason was that we wanted everyone to consciously sign a document representing a commitment on both sides. That way they would understand what their responsibilities were, as well as what they would receive for discharging them."

Depending on specific needs and special considerations, an employment contract usually includes some or all of the following stipulations:

- Term or duration of employment.
- Description of duties.
- Base salary.
- Sign-on bonus.
- Performance bonuses of various kinds.
- Medical, dental, and life insurance.
- Relocation expenses (including company purchase and disposition of the old residence and/or company assumption of closing costs of the new residence).
- Low- or no-interest loans.
- Equity and/or stock options.
- Periodic payment of company-related expenses of various kinds.
- Luxury perks, such as limousines or club memberships.
- Contingency clauses (those good old golden parachutes) in the event of company ownership change.
- Severance conditions (amount, frequency, and duration).
- Contract termination conditions (both for employee and employer).

The best book available for negotiating an advantageous employment deal is John Tarrant's *Perks and Parachutes* (and revised with Paul Fargis in 1997), which contains thorough advice on both contract preparation and negotiations. One important area covers a reluctance on the part of some employers to initiate employment contracts at all. Tarrant recommends minimizing the apparent risk to the employer of putting your arrangement on paper. "Management views an employment contract as something negotiated with people who human resource jargon calls the 'nonexempt' ranks, the wage-and-hour workers," he writes. "Because the word 'contract' is linked to the collective bargaining process, the corporate view is that there is something unseemly about a manager's asking for one." Tarrant argues that you don't have to call it a contract and the employer doesn't have to acknowledge that it's a contract. A memorandum or letter of agreement is all you're looking for, as long as your agreement includes a written record for your files.

The Nitty Gritty

Most candidates feel at a disadvantage when they reach the compensation negotiation stage. Indeed they are at a disadvantage, but the reason is more illusory than real.

IRA v. 401(k)

Q I'm 55 and leaving my job soon. Can I take a 401(k) distribution without penalty?

A Absolutely. Unlike money in an IRA, which you can't touch until you're 59 1/2, 401(k) funds are yours when you reach 55. All that's required to avoid paying the 10 percent withdrawal penalty is that you leave your job in the year that you turn 55 or later. Note: Penalty-free does not mean tax-free.

Should you decide to return to the working world next year, you can still tap that 401(k). You don't have that liberty, though, with 401(k)s that are lying around from previous jobs. To get around this barrier, roll those old 401(k)s into your current employer's plan before you retire. Most companies allow this, but you should check the specifics of your plan.

—Alex Frangos
The Wall Street Journal

Most of us think it unseemly somehow to grovel for dollars. Many feel it crass—even selfish—to bargain for a better financial position. Instead of assuming a strong selling position to negotiate most effectively, then, the candidate is weakened by succumbing to psychological vulnerability.

Never begin salary negotiations until you are relatively certain you have a job offer. When asked about the compensation package you received in your last job, answer concisely, including all bonuses and perks. If you feel you were exploited or underpaid, don't even insinuate it. Playing victim is certain to backfire on you.

If you know what salary range is being offered, and the midpoint is slightly above what you were making, this is the most ideal situation. To the question, "What kind of money were you expecting to make?" You might answer, "Well, my package at Kreeko was $110,000. From the way you describe this job I'd say it would be worth about $125,000." This is not unreasonable. You're asking for roughly a 10-percent raise, and would appear to be worth it.

But let's say the job appears to be a bit of a stretch in the eyes of your prospective boss, yet you're sure you could handle it. The response to that same question might be: "I'm sure I can do the job, but I realize that _____ (mention a specific or two) might be new to me. I'd be willing to start at $110,000—what I was making at Kreeko. Then if in three months I were meeting your expectations, let's say you raise my base to $125,000. If I haven't met your expectations by that time, I'll leave."

This puts you at risk, but in a healthy kind of way. You are demonstrating the courage of your convictions in an all-or-nothing proposal that will almost certainly elevate your candidacy to an offer. Don't make such a proposal, however, unless you mean it and intend to follow through. Empty bravado will have you back on the street within three months. The risk is less than total, though, because company policy, especially in larger companies, probably precludes such ad hoc agreements. Still, just making the proposal will cause your future boss to be less doubtful about your ability, and perhaps lead to a more generous offer.

Try not to get boxed into a specific figure. Always talk in $5,000 to $10,000 ranges. If the interview has gone superbly, aim high and then negotiate. If you are in doubt about the range the employer is considering and are asked about your salary expectations, answer the question with one of your own. "I'm glad you brought up the subject of compensation. What range did you have in mind for the job?" Then negotiate from there.

The fact that you are currently without a paycheck, if such is the case, is no reason to enter negotiations with any lower opinion of your dollar value than if a headhunter had called about this opening when you were happily employed. The following scene from the *Interview to Win* videotape (slightly adapted for our purposes) shows one way to get through this situation:

> **Interviewer:** Well, it's been a long process, Gordon, but we'd like to offer you the marketing manager's job.
>
> **Candidate:** I'm delighted.
>
> **Interviewer:** What would you say to a base of $91,000?
>
> **Candidate:** Actually, I'm a bit disappointed.
>
> **Interviewer:** Well, we're talking about a performance bonus that should run another 15 to 20 percent if things go the way we hope they will. I should have mentioned that at the outset.
>
> **Candidate:** Still, that's only a five percent increase over my Systems International salary. A little less, actually.
>
> **Interviewer:** Well, what did you have in mind?
>
> **Candidate:** I was really expecting something in the low six figures—plus the bonus.
>
> **Interviewer:** I'm afraid that's out of the question. There has to be some growth built into the range for possible raises at review time.

Candidate: Well, maybe there's some give in that area. Is it possible for the review to be moved back to three months?

Interviewer: We're pretty locked in there, I'm afraid. Company policy is a six-month review after hire, and annually thereafter. No exceptions. You know, considering the fact that you don't have a paycheck at all right now, I think this is quite a generous offer.

Candidate: Terry, I don't think that's a factor. I have a lot to offer you, irrespective of why I am available for this position right now. I'm still very interested, and I think my management skills, telemarketing accomplishments, and investment banking exposure make me the ideal candidate for the job.

Interviewer: Well, we're obviously very interested in you or I wouldn't have made an offer in the first place.

Candidate: Well, how about this? If I were to receive a sign-on bonus, it wouldn't disrupt your salary structure for this level and it could go some distance toward making up the differential.

Interviewer: What did you have in mind?

Candidate: $15,000?

Interviewer: (Pause.) I think I could get you 10.

Candidate: You've got a deal.

Interviewer: That's great.

The candidate in the video kept four crucial points in mind during his negotiations:

1. He remained flexible, and looked for alternatives rather than insist on changing what turned out to be a frozen base salary for the position.
2. He handled the reference to his out-of-work status without being defensive and instead put it in a positive light.
3. He took the opportunity to restate his major accomplishments.
4. He described his goals in terms that would benefit the employer as well as himself.

Never make a decision at the interview—whether it's your first, second, or third. Say: "I appreciate your offer and will give it serious consideration. May I call you by Tuesday with my decision? By the way, will you be putting that in writing?" This gives you a chance to weigh any other serious offers, and also to reflect more thoroughly on this one. During this interview you may come up with a question that affects your decision, and even the composition of the job itself. (The example shown in the *Interview to Win* video, telescoped into a "same-day" decision, was structured to give a beginning, middle, and end to the simulation.)

The Incredible Shrinking Stock Option

"The dot-com craze threw conventional practice out the window: Stock options were given to every employee, including many who didn't understand what stock options were, and any company gave out stock options as a way of hiring talent on the cheap.

"It's not surprising that there have been claims made by employees against dot-coms about stock options. Employees who were promised fabulous wealth for working around the clock in low-paying jobs are now finding themselves out of work because their employers are out of business—or if they're lucky, they have a job but their stock options are essentially worthless. As a result they're angry, disillusioned, and looking to blame someone."

—Nick Crincoli, new-media specialist
Morrison & Foerster (Los Angeles-based law firm)

Before you jump at a generous offer, look carefully at the flip side. Don't give up in potential and prestige what you might be gaining in a monthly paycheck. Analyze the entire compensation package, including benefits and perks, to be sure that a lower salary with excellent fringe benefits may indeed not yield more in the long run. Ask your accountant to steer you through the stickier issues.

If you consider this position as a plateau to greater professional rewards down the road, be sure the experience and accomplishments you stand to gain aren't of greater intrinsic value than a higher paying position that my weaken your next resume.

When all the evidence is in, count on your instincts and gut reaction to deliver a decision in your best interests.

Chapter 8

Making the Most of Your New Job

"A man is a success if he gets up in the morning and gets to bed at night, and in between he does what he wants to."

—Bob Dylan

The journey from the day you left your last job to where you are now represents a learning experience you won't soon forget. It is likely that there are positives that came out of your journey—tactics you used, decisions you made—that you can store for future reference. You now know more about yourself, both good and bad, than you did way back then. You've probably eliminated some of the "bad," perhaps including one or more of the problem areas that caused you to leave your last job. If you have done your homework you will have addressed all of the factors within your control.

Still, there are a few protective measures you should consider. Let's hope the preparations you've taken have nullified any of the possible "misfit" problems described in Chapter 2, as well as any fears you have about burnout and plateauing, at least for the next several years.

Take Your "Job Pulse"

Get in the habit of monitoring your job performance and progress on a regular basis. This doesn't mean just tracking the successful completion of assignments you've been given, but continually evaluating your relationships with the people around you: subordinates, peers, and superiors. Learn to assess your ability and willingness to anticipate and solve problems within your sphere of influence.

Ask for Feedback

Without appearing to be paranoid about it, solicit opinions from a colleague you've come to trust about the way you are working your way onto the team. Ask for a meeting

Making Your Stars Shine Brighter

Searching for ways to help your top performers become stars? Here are three ways to nurture your best and brightest.

1. *Work the crowd.* Keep your "A" players stimulated and close to the action by rotating them through your most mission-critical departments. Jeffrey Fox, author of *How to Become a Great Boss* (Hyperion, $16.95), offers an example: "If sales is the heart and lung machine of the company, make sure your star earns his stripes in sales or he will never have credibility with that part of the organization." When top jobs open up, the stars will have a broad base of knowledge—and admirers.

2. *Give them a stage.* Vijay Govindrarjan of Dartmouth's Tuck School of Business suggests giving junior execs a pool of capital for small-scale experimentation. By handing over scarce funds, you're telling your future stars that you respect their ideas. Even if those ideas fail, you gain a window into how they think.

3. *No surprises.* Find out if your stars even want a top job. CEOs often don't communicate their long-term goals for fear of creating overly inflated egos. Theat's not necessarily smart, says William C. Byham, consultant and co-author of *Grow Your Own Leaders* (Financial Times Prentice Hall, $29). If your protégé's aspirations lie elsewhere, you could lose him unexpectedly. Honesty puts you both on the same page and tells the employee that you want to help him succeed on his own.

—Julie Sloane
Fortune Small Business

with your boss a month or so before your review date to assess your progress. If you can time your meeting to coincide with the completion of a particularly good report or sale, so much the better. Occasionally you'll get an opportunity for a drink or a meal with your boss alone, either in town or on the road. This is a good time to work your way around to a "How am I doing?" query to see if there are ways you can improve your attitude, performance, or a particular relationship. Be subtle, and don't appear either overanxious or overly solicitous.

Are You Ready for Your Close-Up?

These days every executive who occasionally speaks for his company needs to be good at TV. You have to be smooth in your delivery and sharp in your comebacks—and do it live, face-to-face with an interviewer. Are you ready for your 15 minutes of fame? Here are six tips from the best media trainers in the business.

1. *Be a great storyteller.* The TV journalist asks you a question, and you deliver what sounds like a memorized, scripted, answer. Big mistake. Michelle Smith of M Strategies consulting in Dallas warns her clients never to deliver a canned response to a question. "Use descriptions, share anecdotes, and be conversational," Smith says. "The journalist's take-away should be, 'Company X is an innovative company.' But you would never *say* 'We are innovative.' That would sound like you're reading from a brochure."

2. *It's not a conversation, it's a presentation. Acting* conversational is one thing. Making the mistake of thinking that an interview is just another chat over a cup of coffee is quite another, says Lee Duffey, president of Atlanta's Duffey Communications: "It's when people are lulled into a sense of camaraderie that they say things they have no business saying. Remember your message. It's more like a job interview or a sales presentation than a conversation.

3. *Take your cue from CNN Headline News.* "So many people are used to standing in front of their teams providing proof after proof in order to justify a decision or explain an accomplishment. Then they do that on camera, and you can just see the interviewer's eyes glaze over," says John Radewagen, vice president of corporate communications at the San Jose-based Hoffman Agency. "I teach people to start at the top and give the conclusion first. Start with the headline, and don't get lost with the proof points."

4. *Be provocative, be passionate.* It's not always bad news when a reporter comes knocking. So don't play the victim or clam up out of fear. "Have something of substance to say," says Duffey. "Don't be afraid to be controversial, as long as you can back it up. Make them want to interview you again."

5. *Hit softballs out of the park.* "Think of an opening and closing anecdote to illustrate your message." That way, if you get a softball lead-in, you can get your message across instead of just saying,

Are You Ready for Your Close-Up?
(cont'd.)

"Thanks for having me here," says Radewagen. The same rule applies at the end of an interview: "When they ask you, 'Is there anything else you'd like to add?' remember that you *always* have something to add," he says. "It's an open invitation."

6. *The mike is always on.* "Even if the light on top of the camera isn't on, the audiotape is usually still rolling," warns Smith. "There's no such thing as 'off the record,'" agrees Duffey. It's the comment that you share "just between us" that is most likely to end up as the voice-over lead-in to the video package—and get you in hot water with your shareholders.

—Alison Overholt
Excerpted from *Fast Company*

Record Your Accomplishments

Make a copy of every good report, memo, letter, or proposal that earned the company money, reduced costs or expenses, solved problems, or resulted in departmental or company growth. Then, when you want to construct another resume, some of your more easily forgotten achievements can be immediately retrieved.

Master "Crossover" Skills

Executives with more than a single specialty can increase their value to the company, particularly in smaller companies. If you can step in to an emergency or "peak performance" situation able to solve problems others can't, your stock will go up, and you will be considered for assignments or promotions not previously open to you. If you're currently in sales management in a healthcare products company, with little opportunity to use your M.B.A. or your engineering background, look for ways to volunteer your services to the operations people. (However, get your boss's approval, and be sure you avoid peak sales seasons, at which time you will of course be expected to pull your department's load, not looking for work outside the department.) Such efforts need by definition to be seen as a win-win for the company, rather than a self-serving exercise by an unusually ambitious department head.

Become a Better Interviewer

Attracting, identifying, evaluating, and hiring the best people is a skill set few managers have. This is true because managers are not often encouraged to develop their interviewing skills. Often a first impression, an amusing war story, or shared experiences are as rigorous as the interviewing experience gets. More hiring mistakes are made because of incomplete, improper, or inefficient interviewing than any other reason.

Many CEOs and senior managers fail to recognize that interviewing and evaluating prospective employees is an integral part of a manager's job. Even in larger corporations where the hiring process is usually both formal and effective, little training is conducted for line managers (where you must choose a trusted lieutenant from the half dozen candidates screened by HR and passed on for your winnowing). It isn't enough for you to be told only that these are the best of the lot. You need to know why they're the best—as well as why the candidates who came close did *not* make the cut. Arrange to spend enough time with the top recruiter—several sessions, if necessary—and find out how and why she does what she does. Ensure that your evaluating criteria and hers are compatible so that good people don't fall through the cracks.

Surviving a Corporate Upheaval

A corporate takeover, merger, or reorganization doesn't have to mean your undoing. If it happens (again), here are a few tips to help you come out ahead:

- *Network early.* As soon as you begin to hear rumors of an impending shakeup, it's time to tap into your professional network. Call business friends an associates to see what jobs are open for which you might qualify and that you would be interested in. Also, let people know you're looking around and that you may be available soon.

- *Start negotiating.* If drastic change seems imminent, try to negotiate a contract that will provide you with a temporary income in case the company's ownership changes hands. If a golden parachute is not an option, see if you can at least make a deal that will guarantee maximum severance pay. Many companies in transition are afraid enough of massive defections that they will offer incentives for staying on, at least until the situation crystallizes.

- *Investigate a transfer option.* If you work for a large company, you may be able to save your skin simply by transferring to a different department or division. Under no circumstances, however, should you pass on a resume until you have thoroughly investigated the target opportunity for possible political repercussions.

A Promotion Freeze—But Just for Me!

Dear Annie:

In the midst of heavy layoffs, our CEO announced that there would be a hiring-and-promotion freeze until business picks up. Fine. I was prepared to hunker down, work hard, and outlast the slowdown. Then last week, a company-wide e-mail congratulated a coworker on a promotion, and I just learned that another colleague has a new title too. I feel that all the extra work I've been doing, for no recognition, is futile. Should I ask what's up, or will that make me look like a sore loser and not a team player?

—Ticked Off

Dear T.O.:

In this, as in so much else, what matters is not so much what you say as how you say it. "Stay focused on your goal," suggests Deborah Bright, Ph.D., a Manhattan-based executive coach (*www.drbright.com*). "If you just demand an explanation, you will sound like a whiner, and it won't get you anywhere." Frame your request for information in a positive way. Go to your boss and say something like, "I'm really glad to see that there have been some promotions lately, in spite of these tough times, and I'd like to talk to you about what I can do to be considered for one of them. Have the conversation as soon as possible. Says Bright: "Sitting around stewing about this isn't good."

—"Ask Annie" (Anne Fisher)
Excerpted from *Fortune*

- *Consider staying.* While it is true that more than half the executives in acquired companies seek other jobs within a year of the takeover, the possibility exists that greater challenge and opportunity exist where you are. One study indicates that 43 percent of managers who stay on after a turnover are promoted.

Spread Your Wings

Broaden and enrich your professionalism through activities beyond the scope of your position. Join and become active in functional or industry organizations. Arrange to speak or write about topics in your field that interest you and that you know about.

Volunteer for company, community, or industry projects or trade show workshops that will improve your visibility. Your first attempts may make you a bit uncomfortable, but stay with it. Your self-confidence will grow substantially with every new experience.

Much success utilizing your potential to the fullest extent.

Appendix A

Q&A

The following exchanges are selected from questions received and answered by the author over the past several years, both from his Website, *www.job-bridge.com*, and from career-related sites for which he served in a "guest expert" capacity (among them MedSearch.com—now part of *www.monster.com*—and *www.6figurejobs.com*). This selection has been organized by content related to specific chapters of the *Executive Job Search Handbook*, and is typical of the concerns and problems faced by job seekers from a wide variety of industries and disciplines.

You'll meet people here suffering age discrimination, burnout, victimization by bullying employers, and frustration because their career marketing plans are not getting them interviews and job offers. Look through all of the exchanges, if you can take the time. You may well find a situation that mirrors your own, or perhaps offers a solution you can use to improve your marketing campaign.

Chapter 2

Q I've been looking to switch jobs because I am very unhappy in my current situation. I have been offered what seems like an ideal opportunity: to work on a freelance basis for three months for my old boss, which would provide a steady salary but allow me flexibility to look for another job. It also would allow me to get back to the industry to which I would like to return.

However, this is a very busy time in my current job. We're hiring for another spot, so we are very overwhelmed. I am the person designated to train the new person when hired. Not only that, we are planning an important conference as well.

I would hate to leave on bad terms here, and if I left now, that certainly would be the case. However, this is a great opportunity and I'd hate to pass it up. There really is no compromise on the start date for the freelance work, because they need me ASAP.

Please let me know what you would advise.

A If there is a way to juggle the two situations, that would be the ideal way out. You'd maximize the opportunity to get back into your old industry (as well as list a transitional job on your resume that positions you perfectly for a return.) At the same time you'd be salvaging your current situation and using a "double paycheck" to hedge against the possibility that it might take you six months rather than three to find the right job back in your previous industry.

If there is to be a tilt, however, I'd make it toward the area you want to be in, rather than the situation that is turning you off. Accept the freelance job. It represents an unexpected opportunity for you to get back where you want to be. Take your old boss into your confidence. Let him know about your conflict, and ask him to be both a reference and a resource for you to get a full-time job as soon as you complete the assignment for him. (Let him know that you would be receptive to additional freelance assignments until you land a full-time position.)

If it happens that doing both jobs begins to affect the quality of your performance at your current job, my advice would be to quit–to be certain your freelance job gets done to your ex-boss's satisfaction. Granted, this would be a relatively high-risk decision. If you don't make it, though, and are forced to remain in an industry you dislike intensely, you may be even more unhappy in a couple of years than you are now. If you do quit, be candid with your current boss; offer to work part-time or freelance to complete those responsibilities that don't interfere with your ability to complete the freelance job satisfactorily. If your offer is rejected, apologize, wish your current boss well, shake hands, and leave to do what is best for you.

Q I'm in the process of transitioning to a new position within my company and would like your advice on the contents that should be "standard" with a transition package.

I am currently the team leader of business proposals for testing services, and our customer base is internal product development and information technology service organizations. My interest is to leave my post in as organized a fashion possible. The transition process I am considering involves several meetings to review and discuss a transition document I am developing. I would appreciate your insight as to pertinent information for the document, and any additional suggestions.

A Your situation may be extremely company-specific, in which case what I write will be of little help. Nevertheless, here are a few obvious considerations:

- Try to anticipate problems your successor might encounter and devote adequate space in your transition document specifying ways to prepare for him or her.
- Categorize and prioritize all foreseeable assignments and situations.
- Leave detailed directions as to where relevant files can be found, and who outside the department might be considered useful source persons for specifically described situations.
- Conduct a meeting with your staff to pass out appropriate "well dones," both generic and specific, and give them some idea of what to expect in the coming months. If you know who your replacement will be, provide an introduction to your people—a live one, if appropriate and if it can be arranged.

Q I am 42, and have been a design engineer for 20 years. My specialty is designing high-precision robotic systems. I have no degree, but do have 25 years experience in my field. My company is growing and reorganizing, and I have had a new boss for exactly one month now, who is about to review me. I earn $82K base, and grossed $97K last year with overtime. My new boss thinks I earn too much. (I was also Design Manager with 21 direct reports for about five years a few years ago.) I think I deserve a $95K base, but he said, "Are you kidding?"

On my 20th anniversary I got no praise or recognition from my managers, although a couple of customers have patted me on the back. From my boss I get only lectures. (I think I intimidate him.)

Should I stay and bear it (which is eating me up inside), go to the higher-ups, or plan to get out of there within the year? I need to provide for my family, and cannot take less money. I need to progress and be free of idiots who don't appreciate what I do for them and don't have a clue as to what I really do.

I know this has been a long question, but I could have gone on for another 100 pages, and just wanted to give you an overview. Thanks for any advice you may have.

A From what you've written and without any additional information, I'd recommend your leaving your present company as soon as possible, but not without first finding another job.

I'd say you are justifiably bitter, but your job now is to put together a job search campaign to offer your services to one of your competitors, without badmouthing your present employer. This is *crucial*. You can legitimately say you are not being challenged, or that new management has changed the ground rules in a way you cannot support, but you must offer as a reason your "professional growth." (With 20 years at the company, it's not as though you're going to be labeled a job-hopper.)

Don't get into personalities or any specifics about the politics involved, no matter how sorely tempted you may be. And keep a few friends in the company at levels above you (one or more to whom you reported, ideally), because you're going to be asked for references there, and one of them won't be your current boss, for sure. Without good references, your chances of getting a job as good as the one you have decrease markedly.

Stay patient, and work on your new job search evenings and weekends until you find the right opportunity. Good luck.

Chapter 3

Q I am looking to transition from the eBusiness industry. While it is a dynamic industry, I do not feel that I am well suited for it in terms of my technical expertise. I would like to find a senior level sales/marketing account management type of position in another industry that has the same kind of potential (perhaps organizational behavior services or something like that).

A To give yourself the best chance, focus on one industry at a time, researching each as thoroughly as your resource base will allow. (By the way, "organizational behavior services or something like that" is a career direction that you'll need to narrow somewhat.) First, talk to at least a half dozen successful individuals in each targeted industry to determine the extent of your prospective fit. Find out what the job is "really like," whether there is a current need for people with your skill sets and background, and what kinds of career paths you might expect. If the answers suggest a "go," construct a resume that specifically positions you within each targeted industry, as best you can.

Q I'm a manufacturing operations manager who has worked with the same company 25 years. During this time I've held supervisory, project leader, and managerial positions. I am currently seeking a career change and have submitted several resumes to governmental agencies in Washington, D.C. What advice could you give in effecting a change?

A First of all, make it your business to learn enough about each governmental agency that interests you to find out which of them offer positions that dovetail with your strengths and interests. In addition to writing the customary application letters, establish personal contacts with individuals in the agency (not necessarily those in a position to hire you, but anyone who can help you determine whether you're looking in the right place). If making such "cold calls" is a strategy new to you, it may take a bit of practice to develop a comfort level that eventually leads to results. But keep trying—that in itself will help make it work.

Q I am an 18-year vet of new business start-ups focusing in technology, Internet, and call center industries. My responsibilities have been cross-organizational. I have the opportunity to cash out equity in my current situation and move on. Based on my background, where should I focus my efforts?

A You're in an excellent position. Take your time as you determine the best next move. If you are sufficiently capitalized and are entrepreneurially inclined, you may want to consider starting your own consulting firm. Take several months, if you need them, to identify a niche market that would reward a problem-solver with your cross-organizational background. Determine whether you should go it alone, or partner with a colleague who possesses complementary skills and background. Then develop a business plan. But whether you decide to work for yourself or for someone else, focus your efforts in a direction that reflects your interests. You've earned the right to have some fun in your next job.

Q I owned a successful computer firm for more than 12 years. I now work for a large corporation but miss the entrepreneurship. I purchased a domain name and have an excellent idea for a niche Website for network professionals but I do not have the time to develop the Web software I need in order to make this venture work. I don't have the money to outsource the programming talent, so I am looking for investors to free me from the job I have so that I can fully focus on my venture. The job I have is extremely demanding but also pays very well. Any ideas?

A Carve out some weekend and evening time to continue developing the software— or farm it out to a developer you trust. The danger exists that if you turn the project over to investors at this formative stage you'll lose control of it by not bringing enough to the table. Invite investors in at a point when they (and you) can see the final product(s) more clearly, which—not incidentally—will tend to increase your equity and financial return.

Q I am in my late 30s and have developed a significant resume with established blue chip names and smaller firms, domestically and internationally. For the past seven or so years, my success has come as an independent consultant, business development expert, and relationship manager at the most senior levels. Yet, it seems that this is being discounted to some extent as I seek to return to the regular corporate path. How should I best capture and describe such independent experience on my resume and in my cover letter?

A Solicit testimonials from those clients willing to write them. Or, write them yourself and ask individual clients, "Is this what you recall being your problem, and my solution to your problem?" Then put names to any testimonials clients are willing to go public with, and sign others simply "Fortune 1000 manufacturing firm" or whatever. This tactic can easily be incorporated into your resume and cover letters.

Q I am a successful entrepreneur who wishes to reenter the corporate world. In a downsizing and least-cost-alternative scenario utilized by many companies, how can multifunctional experience and accomplishments be presented to one's advantage?

A You have at least two alternatives: If your interest is in working for a relatively large corporation (where specialization is highly valued), you will have to sublimate your versatility and focus on a single function you like and at which you excel—sales and marketing, for example. For situations in smaller companies and startup situations, your wide-ranging background will give you a distinct advantage. One option: Use your entreprenerurial skills to leverage an initial consultant contract into an offer of full-time employment.

Chapter 4

Q I am a practicing architect, urban planner, and energy consultant. For the last two decades I have been involved with my field, my colleagues, and my practice. I have reached a point where I would like to "come out of the cold."

The problem I seem to have is selling my services to a firm, as being an architect puts me on the "short side" of the equation. As a consequence I have been spending my time exploring parallel fields—where I know the remuneration is far better. I have poked around with land development firms, which are quite difficult to spot, to see how I could fit in. I have also explored the facilities management field.

Perhaps my resume is not properly focused. But I do feel that it should not be the primary sales tool; I should be that. Please advise.

A Yes, it is true that you should be the primary sales tool, but your resume has to pre-sell you until such time as you are able to schedule a face-to-face meeting. Prepare separate resumes directed to land development companies and facilities management companies, respectively. You need to write specific Objective and Summary sections for each, and then resequence those entries in your Experience section that highlight the skills, accomplishments, and responsibilities that reflect hot buttons for each of the two fields.

Q I am a NASA program manager working in the aerospace industry in Denver. I am having a difficult time transitioning to the commercial IT world. I work primarily on computers and software; however, this experience is on space programs exclusively. I have a B.S.E.E. and a Ph. D. in business management. I think my resume must intimidate people because I have had very few inquiries when I e-mail it or post it to organizations. Any suggestions?

A My guess is that you haven't spent sufficient time retooling your resume for the private sector. You are justifiably proud of your considerable NASA accomplishments, but the organizations to which you post your resume may not be able to visualize your working anywhere *but* at NASA. Take a little time to research three or four organizations that interest you. Find out how you might fit in with each of them—specifically, what problems they have that you might solve. Talk to one or more employees at these companies to learn the language of the industry (which may differ from the public sector language in ways you do not yet know). Use this research as a matrix for the kinds of changes you make on your resume.

Chapter 5

Q I hear from many firms that wish to sell me their services that they have researchers who can locate hidden jobs. I am general counsel for a large manufacturer. Do professionals have access to a hidden market or is this just a ploy to retain the firm's services?

A The "hidden job market" is hidden only to those who don't do sufficient research to unearth this largely unadvertised bumper crop of openings. There is no need to advertise, after all, if qualified candidates are available for interviews. These jobs are filled by people who do their homework and are tapped into the various networks available to them. And they are usually filled quickly, because the candidates who learn of them are not in competition with hundreds of other job seekers who respond to a single ad. Job seekers who do this necessary preliminary work have the whole field to themselves.

Q I have been looking for an executive level position for a couple of months. I receive a lot of phone calls from recruiters and from companies that say they are going to call me back, but never do. Am I doing something wrong?

A I'll assume that when you say you "receive a lot of phone calls from recruiters," you mean in response to calls you have originated. If you receive more than a trickle of unsolicited phone calls from recruiters, it is because you are a candidate in demand—but for some reason aren't saying the right things in response to their qualifying questions. In such calls, help the recruiter establish that you are a viable candidate by specifying the degree to which you match the job in question, after it has been described to you. On the other hand, screen yourself out of contention when it is clear that the job is not for you. (A recruiter will appreciate your candor—and record it accordingly.) If you have been out of work a couple of months, your overeagerness may be reflected in your voice—and is turning off your callers. As a general rule, recruiters avoid unemployed candidates, because their clients expect them to find "winners." If you're out of work, don't rely on recruiters. Instead, develop your own self-marketing skills.

Q I'm a molecular pathology biologist, and have worked in this field for more than three years. I am looking for a job abroad. Please guide me as to where and how I should apply.

A Without either education or experience in your targeted country (or countries), your chances of getting a job abroad are virtually nil. However, if you have friends or relatives in these countries who will give you a base of operations until you get familiar with your professional and cultural surroundings, your possibilities improve.

Q I am a multilingual high-level executive with 20 years of international sales, marketing, and operations experience in hi-tech communications equipment. This includes wireless, broadband, audio/video/data/voice, ATM, HDTV, and digital—all the latest industry "buzzwords." I have a marketing buddy with a similar background, yet we have been looking for a new opportunity for months and not even getting interviews. I have asked several recruiters if my resume is appealing, and have been told that it is outstanding. So the question is, if companies are supposedly prepared to be competitive in the future by hiring individuals with global experience and broad-based knowledge of high technology, why are we still looking? Is the answer that hiring managers are so afraid of hiring of the exceptionally qualified?

A After months of frustrating job search, it is understandable that you begin to point a finger at the hiring managers themselves. (You're not totally wrong, by the way.) There are executives out there capable of this level of paranoia and who feel threatened by superior candidates. But not only are they in the distinct minority, most corporate hiring practices include sufficient checks and balances to preclude such counterproductive shenanigans.

By the way, you won't get a high level of constructive criticism regarding your resume by simply asking if it is "appealing." The recruiters are busy, and will answer "yes" just to get you off the phone. Get some help from a pro.

Q I have been working on repositioning myself and getting placed in a new job for more than 18 months. I have re-tooled my resume at least six times, and am always willing to fine-tune it toward the prospect. I have had at least 12 headhunters, some of whom were good, some of whom were barely breathing. I have sent out over 700 resumes. Most of them included a cover letter that was personalized, if not written for the position in mind. I have sent blind letters to CEOs, answered ads in the papers, listed myself on many Internet boards and services.

I have had some good interviews, and most of them have given me positive responses, but I can't get anyone to move off the dime. No amount of pressure—subtle or unsubtle—seems to work, and I am getting increasingly frustrated.

I am well-educated, and have 17 years experience in my field. I work in media, and have a cross-pollination of traditional and electronic media which I have mastered, and

I simply can't get my prospects to take me on. I can't believe it is simply because I am older than most applicants, but I am sure that is part of it. (I am 46.) I can't believe it is that I am in a rather esoteric aspect of the business, but that may be it too. Most Internet and new media positions seem to be heavily weighted toward those with an M.B.A., which I do not have. Yet in my experience, I know I am as good or better than most of the people I have met in the business.

I have taken courses and advice from HR people and recruiters, and do not seem to have a personality conflict with most potential employers–but seem to have just bad luck. And it is getting tiresome!

In the last three jobs I applied for with a degree of surety that they were mine, the first put the position on hold "indefinitely." The second did away with the position altogether before they could hire anyone. The next did away with the department. I am beginning to feel like the kiss of death. But I have been consulting (in the roller coaster fashion of all consultants' workloads), and have been doing well at each individual job, with very pleased clients and good product coming out.

Have you any idea what is going on? Is it just a numbers game? Why does it take so long for the right combination to hit? I am up for any consideration about this situation.

A Well, let's see. First, I will give a couple of observations, and then attempt to answer your questions.

- *"I have had at least 12 headhunters, some of whom were good, some barely breathing."* That's about right. But here's the point: If you've been looking for 18 months, headhunters are your *last* resort. Those you call "good" were being nice to you. Unless you're a perfect match for an assignment they have (which works out to about one time in a thousand), they're a waste of your time other than to send off a resume (think lottery ticket) and then forget about it.

- *"I have sent out over 700 resumes, either electronically, by fax, or snail mail."* Mass mailings are probably the highest-risk, lowest-yield marketing strategy a job seeker can use. You say most of these submissions included a cover letter that was personalized, if not written for the position in mind. Does "personalized" mean you addressed your letter to someone other than "Dear Sir:" and that you mentioned the open position? If so, this is not going to do it. In your situation, "personalized" had better mean learning enough about a target company to be able to propose solutions to problems you have identified through solid research—and can solve.

- The same rings true with your blind letters to CEOs. If by "blind" you mean without referencing a specific job, this is not a bad idea. These should all be well thought out proposals. You should include what you can do for a company you've taken time to learn something about. But if you're writing only to tell them how great you are, and that they can't afford not to hire you, you're wasting your time.

- As to the results of your last three job possibilities, I would agree that you were victimized by circumstances and couldn't have done anything differently to affect the decision. "Is it a numbers game?" you ask. Based on what you have written, I would say yes. But you have been complicit by making it a numbers game of your own. Concentrate on just a handful of target companies at a time, and learn enough about each of them to be able to propose a reasoned rationale for deserving to be on the payroll.

Q I'm currently working at a high-level position abroad and am looking to return home to the United States. Unfortunately, in my current position I'm not able to openly look for another job, and even if I did being abroad complicates things. So my question is this: Where do I find a headhunter who represents individuals, not companies? Please advise.

A By definition, there's no such thing as a headhunter who represents individuals. If you know exactly what you want to do when you return to the States, and what companies would be good prospective matches for your experience and accomplishments, contact the appropriate people and attempt to schedule interviews around your next planned U.S. visit or vacation. There are career consultants who represent individuals, whom you probably can identify with the aid of an Internet search engine.

Q I am a senior manager working on the merger of one of the several Fortune 100 mergers currently in the works. I have indicated a desire to leave when the merger is approved and starts up. This could be as early as this coming November or as late as next April. I am only in the early stage of a search, having just completed my resume, and have begun assembling networking resources. I plan to launch a broadcast campaign to retained search firms as well.

My question is: Is the end of the year a less desirable time to start a broadcast campaign? Does the timing matter for when I send off letters?

A First of all, no, the timing doesn't matter—in fact, the sooner the better. Second, send off letters and resumes to selected recruiters, by all means. (Use the *Directory of Executive Recruiters*, from Kennedy Publications, to qualify recruiters by specialization and geographic coverage.) Your use of the word "broadcast," however, makes me nervous. Broadcast mailings, whether to companies or to recruiters, are far less effective than targeted, well-researched, letters to either. Start at the top of your wish list, and work you way down.

Q I am in the over-50 category and have an impressive resume. It shows a focused and progressive career at four high-profile organizations, has no gaps, and lists ample accomplishments. I have an M.B.A. and a doctorate in business administration, yet I cannot get an interview. Should I consider "dumbing down" in order to be a more attractive candidate?

A You will be an attractive candidate only if you can convince target companies that your impressive background includes tools to help solve their business problems. Some companies believe that older candidates are living in the past and that they think they should be hired for what they have done, rather than what they can do. Research each company with which you have an opportunity to interview to see what problems you can help them solve. Then make that case as best you can. Shift your emphasis from the past to the future and from your needs to those of the target company.

Chapter 6

Q I am thinking about creating a portfolio of all the various projects I have completed with past jobs. I hope to bring this to an interview to further enhance my ability to capture the attention of the employer.

Do you have any tips on how to construct a portfolio properly? When is the best time to hand it to the employer?

A Portfolios are tangible examples of solutions to various problems your resume indicates that you successfully handled. They should include only those projects of specific interest to the target company rather than everything significant you have ever done. Be prepared to walk the interviewer through your specific participation in the project. On the other hand, don't oversell your involvement. But do take credit for everything you *legitimately* were responsible for. If you are asked to mail your portfolio prior to the interview, ask for some indication of exactly what would be most appropriate to include. This may help you focus only on materials of specific interest. When the portfolio precedes you, add written narrative attached by Post-It to each exhibit by way of keeping the reader informed as to context. Where applicable, add, delete, or reemphasize different projects, depending on the situation.

As to timing: Hand the portfolio to the interviewer when you are asked to. If you are not asked, take it out (with the interviewer's permission) to illustrate an answer to a question about your solution to such-and-such a problem. At the end of the interview, ask if it would be helpful for you to leave the portfolio with the company for a few days. If the answer is yes, set a specific day and time to pick it up. This could be a way to "pre-schedule" a second interview.

Q I am a little baffled! I interviewed at a company, after which the CEO looked me in the eye and offered me the job. He indicated that I would have the offer in writing by the end of the week and I never heard from him or the company again. What went wrong?

A Any number of things could have gone wrong. On the off-chance that an honest glitch of some kind occurred, call the CEO and ask first if there is a reason for the "delay" in getting the written offer to you. If the answer is equivocal, or if you aren't able to get through to him directly, you'll know that:

1. Their decision-making process changed.
2. Negative information about your candidacy surfaced from one source or another, perhaps from one of your references.

You have no control over the first alternative, of course—even though the company demonstrated poor communication skills by not getting back to you. If this is the case, just move on and try to put the experience behind you. If company representatives changed their minds after you received the verbal offer, however, try to discover what negative information came to light, as well as its source, (If you learn that a former boss is badmouthing you, for example, find out why, to preclude further poisoning of the well.) If it happens to be one of your references, it is best to eliminate that person from your marketing team, *immediately.*

Chapter 7

Q What's the best way to handle multiple offers? What's the most practical way to compare offers that include bonuses, stock options, benefits, days off, and so forth?

A Handling multiple offers is a matter of timing. Ask for as much time as it will take you to come to a decision, without tipping your hand by asking for too much. If you're waiting for Company B to weigh in before you decide what to tell Company A, you may say you want to talk it over with your spouse face to face before you come to a conclusion. (She's with her folks in Ohio, and won't return until next Thursday.)

List all tangible and intangible reasons to go with one company or the other. And make it a list of equivalent points: What Company A has that Company B (and C, if your fortune is that good) does not. Do your best to weight each point as accurately as you can. If a location question is involved, *www.yahoo.com* has a nifty little feature allowing one to compare two different U.S. cities side by side, point for point. (To show its thoroughness, there are six *Alaskan* cities alone from which to choose.) Comparisons are made in a number of categories under general topics such as finance and economy, real estate, quality of life, education, weather, and salary, among others. From Yahoo's home page, go to "Business&Economy" (Jobs) to "Yahoo careers" to "relocation sources" to "city comparison."

Appendix **B**

Sample Cover Letters

Response to a newspaper or trade journal ad

November 23, 2003

Mr. Ulys S. Yates
Director of Recruitment
Vidatchi Instruments, Inc.
1410 W. Lawndale
Naperville, IL 60110

Dear Mr. Yates:

Your ad for a Senior Analytical Scientist in the *Chicago Tribune* last Sunday is of considerable interest to me. As it happens, those requirements that seem to be of most importance to you match up extremely well with my own credentials. Let me deal with them one by one:

In-depth knowledge of analytical techniques:

As Senior Applications Chemist for the Uniroyal Company I routinely utilize FT, NMR, MS, Gas Chromatography, GC/MS, Infrared, high vacuum line technique, and MALDI-MS.

Working knowledge of computer/instrument interfaces:

For five years as a Senior Engineer for IBM Instruments, I developed new environmental instruments, evaluated analytical instrumentation, and programmed computers in C, C++, Perl, and MDPN.

The areas of responsibility you list make this position of exceptional appeal to me. I currently work closely with customers on-site to develop unique applications and assist in troubleshooting equipment.

As Laboratory Database Manager at Uniroyal, I designed and developed a sophisticated system for managing technical and marketing information using Pascal/Delphi and Tcl/Tk. My Ph.D. is in Inorganic Chemistry from the University of Michigan, and my direct laboratory experience totals 11 years.

I look forward to discussing my candidacy with you in detail, and will call in a week or so to arrange a personal interview, if I have not heard from you in the meantime. My resume is enclosed.

Sincerely,

Stanley Petnuinas

Stanley Petnuinas

Enclosure: Resume

Introduction to an executive recruiter

December 15, 2003

Mr. Allan Sussman
Heidrick & Scruggles
4810 Wilshire Boulevard
Los Angeles, CA 96411

Dear Mr. Sussman:

Thanks for your time on the phone Friday. As you suggested, I have enclosed a copy of my resume for your consideration—as well as described my current situation.

My employer, Andover Development Group Ltd., has sold the majority of its U.S. holdings to Bell Canada Enterprises Development Corporation (formerly Daon Development Corporation. In addition, Andover is in the process of selling a substantial percentage of its Canadian holdings. This will eliminate my position as treasurer once these sales and the related tax compliance work have been completed.

My objective is to join a large company with real estate investment or service interests in its senior tax position, with the responsibility for all aspects of corporate taxation. I would work with the company's executives in formulating and executing tax and financial planning for the business. Additional experience in such a company's financial area would then permit me to move eventually into senior management. I am also interested in joining a company that has international activity, enabling me to become involved in the tax and financial structuring of transactions.

My current salary is a $169,000 U.S. base, with an additional 20 percent bonus potential.

Because my position is being eliminated due to the sale of Andover's U.S. and Canadian holdings, I can provide excellent references regarding my performance. I appreciate your assistance, and will call in a week or so to see if my background might match an assignment in which you are currently engaged, and to arrange a personal meeting to discuss other possibilities.

Sincerely,

John S. Baswell

John S. Baswell
Enclosure: Resume

Third-party introduction to a corporation

September 26, 2003

Mr. Robert J.R. Follett, President
Follett Publishing Company
1010 W. Madison Street
Chicago, IL 60612

Dear Mr. Follett:

Earlier this week I had the opportunity to speak with J.J. Laukaitis, your Vice President for Sales, who told me a little bit about the Executive Editor opening in your Adult Education Department. This position interests me very much, and I believe my background would enable me to contribute significantly to the department's success. According to J.J., there are three aspects of this position on which you place a high priority. Below I have attempted to address each of them by citing examples from my professional experience:

Requirements	My Qualifications
Strong management background in the educational publishing industry:	Nine years with a $500 million publisher of educational materials in a variety of managerial roles, including Manager of Long-Range Planning, Editor-in-Chief, and Managing Editor.
Strategic planning:	Developed a publishing strategy for the science, math, reading, and social studies departments, increasing sales from $17 million to $69.5 million. Programs included ESL components and provisions for under-achieving students.
Staff development:	Hired and trained managers and staff capable in all phases of product development, assuring quality product produced on schedule and to budget.

I welcome the opportunity to discuss this position with you in more detail. I'll call next week to see if you agree that mutual interest could be served by a meeting. Enclosed is my resume.

Sincerely,

Nancy L. Latimer

Nancy L. Latimer
Enclosure: Resume

> Slight career change letter of introduction

October 29, 2003

Mr. Jules Savingard
President and General Manager
WGBH-TV
186 Boylston Street
Boston, MA 02128

Dear Mr. Savingard:

For the past 15 years I have codirected Laminus Productions, a film, television, and audiovisual production company I cofounded to serve clients in publishing, advertising, and other manufacturing and service industries. As you will see on the enclosed resume, my clients include McGraw-Hill, American Express, Young & Rubicam, and Amerada Hess.

My interest at this point in my career is to devote fewer energies to building a business and more to developing product. I have determined that the way to do this is to work with one "client" only—and do it full-time.

This decision is reached from a position of strength: I have eight active clients and a number of additional projects under development. The point is, I am underutilizing my product development skills and believe that I can offer WGBH-TV an experienced, conscientious line producer.

Please look over my resume to see if enough of my skills and accomplishments match your current or imminent needs to warrant a personal meeting. I'll call you in a week or so to get your opinion.

Sincerely,

Robert DeBreaux

Robert DeBreaux
Enclosure: Resume

Appendix C

Sample Resumes

John R. Bennett, SPHR
1480 Allentown Road
Dixmoor, PA 18230
215-864-3181
jrbennett@earthlink.net

Human resources professional experienced and at-ease in both Fortune 200 and smaller environments. Demonstrated ability to function both strategically and tactically. Expertise in installing and re-engineering human resources process. A change agent, with proficiencies in effective communications, team building, and employee and organizational development. Hands-on individual capable of driving the best practices in the areas of staffing, compensation & benefits, employee relations, performance management, and legal compliance. **Fiscally astute manager with a proven track record of generating millions of dollars of expense reduction that flowed directly to the bottom line.**

EXPERIENCE

Strategic Alliance Group, Inc., Philadelphia, PA   **1999 to 2001**

A global boutique consulting firm specializing in business transformation through an e-learning platform.

Vice President, Human Resources

The business plan called for the development of robust on-line learning products. By implementing a best practices staffing model, successfully recruited and hired 135 technical and sales professionals **in less than six months at an average cost per hire of $4,100, which saved the company over $600,000 in recruiting expense.** The projected revenue from the introduction of these three new products represented a 30 percent increase in revenue for the business.

SAG was losing valuable employees. After assessing and overhauling the compensation and benefit programs, **the employee turnover rate was reduced from 18 to 6.9 percent in less than 18** months, reducing recruiting costs but more importantly preserving extremely valuable intellectual capital.

Developed a new performance management system for SAG. This system linked the performance goals of each employee to the organization's strategic goals. This allowed managers to begin having routine dialogues with their employees. As a result, the number of employee-relations issues **were reduced by over 50 percent.**

Mapster, Inc., New York, NY   **1997 to 1999**

The parent of Music Avenue (an on-line music retailer) and the Mapster record label. Acquired during Q2 of 1999.

Vice President, Human Resources

In order to compete with Amazon and CDnow, we needed to quickly add resources to refine our e-commerce platform. **By hiring 100 Web developers and designers quickly, in a highly competitive job** market, we were able to develop rich content and community, and remain competitive in a rapidly changing marketplace.

After significant analysis of our benefit plans and lengthy negotiations with our insurance providers, an immediate decrease of $140,000 in employer health insurance expenses was experienced.

To support the rapid growth of the business, a creative, unusual and efficacious managerial competencies training program was developed. Every manager including the CEO, attended the program. This training enabled management to better handle a wide range of employee/organizational issues. Managers praised the program.

Fundamental Solutions Ltd., Malvern, PA   **1995 to 1997**

A developer of sophisticated asset management systems owned by Ritualistic Scientifics. Acquired by Suroco Systems in 1997.

Vice President. Human Resources

Developed and successfully implemented the first human resources function for this global financial services software provider.

Faced with low employee morale, a corporate culture survey was conducted that facilitated improved cornrnunications between management and employees. Communication tools, including an employee intranet, a monthly company newsletter, and bi-weekly employee meetings were initiated. **As a direct result of this strategy, employee turnover was reduced from 21 to 13 percent in less than a year, which saved the company $250,000.**

In order to maximize the impact of the employee benefit plan budget, a new relationship with brokers and insurance providers was formed. The plans were reviewed, which ultimately reduced the benefit costs, **saving the company $125,000.**

46 billable positions were hired enabling the company to achieve a 15 percent increase in revenue over the prior period.

Crown Consumer Company, Inc., Philadelphia PA   **1991 to 1995**

A Fortune 100 packaging manufacturer headquartered in Philadelphia.

Corporate Manager, Human Resources

Implemented the very first human resources function for this Fortune 100 company with 27,000 employees.

Crown acquired 14 companies with a wide range of compensation, benefits and human resources programs. By analyzing each compensation, benefit and human resources program, a new 401(k) third party administrator was selected and a new plan was created with over $120 million in trust, saving the company over $200,000 annually in administrative fees.

Developed and implemented a broad-banding compensation program that provided consistency between all 14 acquired companies.

Streamlined the human resources information system, selected and installed an enterprise resource planning system, which went live three months ahead of schedule and $150,000 under-budget. This system managed all human resources data for more than 27,000 employees worldwide.

EDUCATION

Master of Business Administration, Finance, Princeton University (1990)
Bachelor of Science, Business Administration, Princeton University (1986)
Senior Professional in Human Resources (SPHR) (1994)
Professional Human Resource Management, Villanova University (1995)
Strategic Human Resources Planning, Cornell University (1992)

PROFESSIONAL AFFILIATIONS AND ACTIVITIES

Past Board Member Society for Human Resources Management.

Consultant to *Fortune Small Business* on human resources policy issues.

Appearance on CNBL *Workplace Forum* discussing trends in employment.

Featured guest on WPGL FM's *Community Forum*, discussing employment and the Internet.

Online resume—Global marketing executive

Brian Lassiter
1432 West Court
Sharon, MA 01763
(978)278-9030
blassiter@aol.com

Accomplished, results-oriented sales and marketing executive with globally progressive leadership for high achievements and positive results

- Excellent interpersonal and team building skills.
- Highly effective strategic planning capability.
- Excellent and extensive global sales and marketing experience.
- Extensive experience in global marketing strategy and tactical execution.
- Experienced in forward thinking global product portfolio development.
- Skilled in global distribution and sales force development.
- Extensive global travel and market knowledge.

PROFESSIONAL HISTORY

2001-2002 CMAI, Inc., Canton, MA
Vice-President, Global Marketing

Responsible for all global marketing functions within a $200M turnaround medical device company. Major accomplishments include restaffing a nonexistent marketing organization, instituting a strategic planning process, instilling all marketing disciplines, and global rebranding of a 100-year-old company. Direct reports inclusive of Global Marketing Product Directors, Conventions Director, and Communications Director. Responsible for multimillion dollar marketing budget.

1998-2001 Reiser Carbomedics, Inc. A Reiser Medica Co., Dallas, TX
Vice-President, Pacific Rim Sales Operations Vice-President, Global Marketing

Responsible for all global marketing functions, clinical affairs, business development, and Pacific Rim sales and distribution operations for a $150 million heart valve organization. Accomplishments include developing alternative distribution channels for the Pacific Rim, developing a five year strategic plan, development of product portfolio strategy, launched five new heart valves, planning and executing an acquisition strategy, and development of United States and European Medical Advisory Boards. Direct reports include, Vice-President Clinical Affairs, Director of Business Development, and Marketing Directors. Responsible for multimillion dollar sales and marketing budget.

1997-1998 Pulmodyne Inc. Barstow, CA
Vice-President, Sales and Marketing

Responsible for all global sales and marketing functions and strategic business alliances for an early stage heart laser organization. Established distributor agreements in all major global markets, including China, Europe, India, Japan, Middle East, South America, and South Korea. Negotiated purchase agreements in some of the world's largest hospitals. Implemented Medical Advisory Board and worked closely with venture capital groups.

Brian Lassiter (page 2)

1993-1997 Pacemaker, Inc. A St. Francis Medical Co. Monterey, CA
Director, Global Bradycardia Marketing

Responsible for all global strategic and tactical product initiatives for a $500 million pacemaker product line. Staff included six U.S. direct reports and a European Marketing Director. Managed all phases of product lifecycle. Responsible for directing all activities of global product communication, education, pricing guidelines, and product launches. Team launched seven new pacemakers, four new pacing leads, and two new programmers. Established five year product plan for all pacemakers, leads, and programmers. Developed bradycardia five year Strategic Marketing Plan. Responsible for multimillion dollar marketing budget.

1986-1993 Medtronic, Inc. Pacing Business Unit. Minneapolis, MN
Global Marketing Manager, 1988 to 1993

Responsible for developing global product strategy and tactics for a $700 million product line of single chamber bradycardia pacemakers. Managed all phases of product life cycle, including feature definition, introduction, pricing, forecasting, and phase-in and phaseout with model mix shift strategies. Developed all global communication, education, and product launch packages for the world's most widely prescribed pacemakers. Product line mix increased annual sales revenues from $350 to $700 million, while contributing to a 15% market share gain in a five year period. Increased average product line selling price by 30%. Responsible for a $2 million product line marketing budget.

Developed and gained Senior Management approval for Medtronic's 10 year bradycardia product plan utilizing the Quality Function Deployment process. Nominated for the Malcolm Baldridge Quality Award. Twice nominated for the Star of Excellence Quality Award. President, Medtronic 300-member Marketing Council.

Regional Marketing Manager, 1986 to 1988, Dallas, TX

Implemented tactical marketing programs for 13 US states.

1984-1986 Warner-Lambert, Inc.
Sales Representative, Dallas, TX

Sales Representative to cardiologists and critical care nurses for thermodilution catheters and cardiac output computers in a five state territory. Top US sales representative.

1981-1984 Travenol Laboratories, Inc.
Sales Representative, Dallas, TX

Sales Representative to cardiovascular surgeons and perfusionists for open heart bypass disposables and capital equipment in a five state territory. Increased market share 15 percent and annual revenue by $3 million in a territory generating $10 million annual revenue.

EDUCATION

MBA Strategic Marketing, University of Central Oklahoma
BS Pharmacy/ Doctor of Pharmacy, University of Oklahoma
United States Marine Corps, Forward Observer
E-5 Platoon Sergeant, Honorable Discharge

James L. Campbell
P.O. Box 541, Springfield, Vermont 05154
Office 802.875.6243, Home 802.875.6304

Objective

Chief Financial Officer, Educational Institution

Summary of Qualifications

More than 30 years financial and operations management experience in the education sector. Visionary leader comfortable addressing details of budgetary constraints as well as long-range planning issues. Demonstrated ability to assess risk and respond appropriately. Proficient troubleshooter in such disparate areas as real estate management, food service delivery, fiduciary obligations, transportation and physical plant. Acted as the "general contractor" to insure that all non-instructional services were being provided and integrated into our master plan.

Experience

Business Manager - July 1994 to Present
Greenwood School: Putnum, Vermont

Responsibilities:

Manage annual budget to assure appropriate allocation and use of resources; supervise outside auditors; manage accounts receivable/payable, and all purchasing. Account collection process using credit bureau data, e-mail, telephone calls, letters, and litigation.

Monitor financial health of the Academy on a continuing basis: Initiate, conduct, and present analyses of various aspects of school finances to assist Board and Headmaster to maximize allocation of school resources.

Serve on and participate in committees of the Independent Schools of Northern New England (ISANNE), the Association of Independent Schools of New England (AISNE), and the National Association of Independent Schools (NAIS); participate on evaluation teams when requested by the New England Association of Schools and Colleges (NEASC).

Manage Academy physical plant to support school's academic residential, and co-curricular needs. Planned and executed athletic, academic, and residential projects totaling over 5 million dollars. Oversee compliance regulations of Environmental Protection Agency and Department of Transportation.

As human resources manager, ensure that proper pay, benefits, and compliance systems are in place to attract, retain, and motivate a strong workforce. Able to terminate employees, when necessary, if progressive remediation plan is not fruitful

Supervise operations of group insurance, pension, vacations, sick leaves, Section 125, and automatic deposit of paychecks.

Oversee compliance of labor laws, wage regulations, ERISA, COBRA, EEO, ADA, and safety with IRS, Immigration and Naturalization Service, Department of Labor, Department of Justice, and Occupational Safety Health Administration regulations.

James L. Campbell/2

Act as Assistant Secretary to the Board, administrative support to Buildings/Grounds and Finance communities, and participate in Strategic Planning Committee decisions.

Selected Accomplishments

Selection and support of good managers. Have identified, selected, and empowered all operations managers; for example, I ensured a foreman was promoted to plant manager; secured an excellent accountant; similarly recruited a creative foodservice manager and promoted a bookstore manager from position of lesser responsibility.

Advanced the use of technology. Initiated installation of campus-wide communications network for computer access and telephone services. Introduced debit card system, electronic time card system, radios for maintenance, telephone call accounting, and Internet services campus-wide.

Balanced budgets. Developed new revenue sources with bus rentals, catering, and student charges, Improved revenue from summer programs, hockey rink, bus rental and other auxiliary enterprises.

Plant project oversight. Supervised or provided support to such projects as Alumni Hall renovation, hockey rink improvements, pottery shop renovation, student center renovation, and upgrade of vehicle fleet.

Secured $2,109,000 tax-exempt bond for capital needs, managed bank relations for seasonal borrowing.

• • •

From 1979 to 1994, held similar staff positions of increasing responsibility (as well as one three-year faculty assignment) at the following New York or New England secondary institutions:

Controller - June 1989 to June 1994
Bennington School: Bennington, Vermont

Business Manager - June 1986 to June 1989
Williston Northampton School: Easthampton, Massachusetts

Business Manager - August 1979 to May 1986
The Wheeler School: Providence, Rhode Island

Education

M.B.A., Finance, and dual major, management January 1980
Syracuse Unversity: Syracuse, New York
B.A., Economics, (minor, business) June 1977
Dean's List, Scholarship Recipient, Dormitory Resident Advisor
Parsons College: Fairfield, Iowa

Community Involvement

Rockingham Area Community Land Trust - President
Independent Schools of Northern New England - Past President
The Grammar School, Putney - Trustee

Print resume—Stock exchange marketing manager

Marcia J. Shin
1871 Fairlane Avenue • Scarsdale, NY 10493 • (914)781-4421
mshin@netscape.com

- In-depth experience in strategy, product management and marketing, from concept to completion.
- Background spans financial services, information providers, communications, professional services and publishing industries; print, electronic, interactive and Web-based products.
- Results-driven leader with solid strategic thinking, analytical, and communications skills.
- Creative and versatile customer-focused team player skilled at leading and motivating others.

Experience

United Financial Services, New York, NY 1994- Present

Managing Director, Planning and Development, Corporate Client Group (2002-Present)

Lead planning and development of business and marketing strategies for new product initiatives designed to support customer retention and new business.

- Directed planning and development of comprehensive training program for highly skilled analysts in a new state-of-the-art market intelligence call center.

Director, Interactive Services, United MarketSite (1998-2001)

Led initiative to create and establish highly visible revenue-generating interactive visitor center and managed P&L responsibility. Directed development, start-up, and all marketing, content, operational and technical functions. Led staff of 24.

- Led strategic planning, concept development, creative strategy, and physical design.
  - ➤ *Achieved aggressive 18-month schedule to start up within strict budget constraints.*
- Directed simultaneous development of diverse interactive and multimedia projects.
- Successfully created awareness and generated business among domestic and international clients.
- Achieved high level of customer satisfaction as shown by market research.
  - ➤ *More than 8 in 10 customers reported that they would recommend MarketSite.*
  - ➤ *Customer service ratings exceeded industry benchmarks.*

Director, United Online, Worldwide Marketing (1996-1998)

Led effort to define, create, and market a leading-edge Web-based product. Integrated developers, consultants, and suppliers into an effective team.

- ➤ *Received United "outstanding achievement" award.*
- Succeeded in identifying and creating a unique, value-added market intelligence service.

➢ *Rated #1 Investor relations Website by National Investor Relations Institute.*

➢ *Won "excellence in communication and graphic design" award (Graphic Design USA).*

➢ *Received record high outstanding quality rating in annual customer survey.*

- Led development of effective marketing strategy to maximize product acceptance.

➢ *Succeeded in penetrating more than 70 percent of target market within six months.*

Represented United as a conference speaker:

- Microsoft's Latin American Enterprise Solutions Conference (May, 1997)

➢ *Presented United Online Website during <u>Microsoft CEO Bill Gates's</u> keynote address.*

- National Investor Relations Institute, "United Seminar" (December, 1997; March, 1998).

Director, Product Management, Issuer Services (1994-1996)

Led planning and development of consulting services marketing plan and information products to support customer retention.

HarperCollins Publishing, New York, NY 1993-1994

Director of Marketing (1993-1994)

Directed planning and implementation of marketing strategies for $20 million publisher of print and electronic professional products. Initiated strategic analysis and recommendation to realign resources. Led to shift from functional management to team orientation.

American Banker - Bond Buyer (Thomson Financial Services), New York, NY 1987-1991

Product Manager (1989-1991)

Managed P&L responsibility for business units that produced conferences ($1.2 million) and publishing products ($1.7 million) for the financial services community. Led development of database publishing system. Repositioned mature product for growth.

➢ *Turned around declining sales trend and achieved 10 percent revenue growth*

NBC Inc., New York, NY 1986-1987

Senior Financial Analyst

Developed monthly financial forecast, annual operating budget, monehly budget analysis, and profit impact analysis. Interacted with executive levels in staff and line management.

Education

Columbia University Graduate School of Business - New York, NY

M.B.A., Finance, 1986

Summer Intem: Analyst, N.Y.C. Dept. of Environmental Protection

Tufts University - Boston, MA

B.S., Cum Laude, Psychology, 1981

Special project: Team research on psychological entrapment

Kent State University Geneva Program - Switzerland (Spring 1980)

Bibliography

Alford, C. Fred, *Whistleblowers: Broken Lives and Organizational Power.* **Ithaca, NY: Cornell University Press, 2002.** About half of all whistleblowers get fired, half of those fired will lose their homes, and most of those will then lose their families too, says the author. This book examines the downside of doing the right thing. It also looks at the ethical and political aspects of whistleblowing, and what the whistleblowers he interviewed have learned from their experiences.

Badaracco, Joseph L. Jr., *Leading Quietly: An Unorthodox Guide to Doing the Right Thing.* **Boston: Harvard Business School Press, 2002.** Executives who choose responsible, behind-the-scenes action over public heroism to resolve tough challenges don't fit the stereotype of the bold, gutsy leader—and they don't want to. In today's fast and fluid business world, nothing is as it seems. A Harvard Business School professor offers eight practical and counterintuitive guidelines for confronting situations in which right and wrong seem to be moving targets.

Collamer, Nancy, *The Layoff Survival Guide: Practical Strategies for Managing the Transition from Pink-Slip to Paycheck.* **E-book:** *www.layoffsurvivalguide.com.* Strategies to preclude a second occurrence. "If your boss didn't want you working flexible hours or telecommuting in the first place, you could be especially vulnerable," she says. Also make sure you're a revenue producer, not a cost center. "Too many women tend to be concentrated in staff areas like marketing or HR. Over time, try to move from a staff position into a line job."

Crowther, Karmen, *Researching Your Way to a Good Job.* **New York: John Wiley & Sons, 1993.** Provides tools and techniques to examine potential employers and jobs, and job-related information on other communities, if you intend to relocate.

Dikel, Margaret Riley, and Frances Roehm, *The Guide to Internet Job Searching.* **Chicago: McGraw-Hill/Contemporary Books, 2002-2003.** How to target the most interesting jobs in the most promising companies, and how to apply for those jobs with confidence–online or on paper.

Encyclopedia of Associations, 2000 edition. **Detroit: Gale Research, Inc. 1994.** More than 22,000 national and international organizations, listed alphabetically. Provides such information as number of members, budget, publications, purpose, and mission. Most specialties in all industries and functions.

Joel, Lewin G., *Every Employee's Guide to the Law.* **New York: Pantheon Books, 2001.** From coping with on-the-job problems to negotiating severance pay, this easy-to-read, concise, and reassuring guide explains everything you need to know about your rights as an employee–and what action you can take if your employer is violating them.

Occupational Outlook Handbook. **Washington, D.C.: U.S. Department of Labor, Bureau of Labor Statistics (2002-2003 Edition).** A nationally recognized source of career information for more than 50 years. Describes what workers do on the job, the training and education needed, earnings, working conditions, and job prospects covering thousands of professional and technical positions.

O'Connor, Patricia, *Woe Is I: The Grammarphobe's Guide to Better English in Plain English.* **New York: G.P. Putnam's Sons, 1996.** Irrefutable advice to eliminate gaffes in either your interview or your resume. As she says in her Introduction, "Whatever your particular boo-boo, *Woe Is I* can fix it without hitting you over the head with a lot of technical jargon. No heavy lifting, no assembly required."

Savageau, David, and Geoffrey Loftus, *Places Rated Almanac: Your Guide to Finding the Best Places to Live in North America.* **New York: Simon & Schuster, 1997.** All 351 U.S. and Canadian metropolitan areas ranked and compared for living costs, job outlook, transportation, higher education, healthcare, crime, the arts, recreation, and climate.

Strunk, William, Jr., and E. B. White (with Roger Angell), *Elements of Style, 4th ed.* **New York: Allyn & Bacon Company, Inc., 2000.** The best "little book" in print on making words count. In just 85 pages, it covers the essentials of word usage, composition, form, style, and commonly misused words and expressions.

Tarrant, John, with Paul Fargis, *Perks and Parachutes, 2nd ed.* **New York: Stonesong Press (Random House), 1997.** The best book available on contract negotiation–what should and should not be part of any employment deal. Includes compensation terms, benefit packages, how job performance is judged, when you can be fired, and your rights after you leave the company.

Useem, Michael, *Leading Up: How to Lead Your Boss So You Both Win.* **New York: Crown Business, 2001.** Do any of your colleagues share your frustration? "There's safety in numbers," writes Useem. "Try to get a group of three or four people together to take the boss out to lunch and address the problem."

Wilson, Robert F., *Better Résumés for Executives and Professionals, 4th ed.* **Hauppauge, NY: Barron's Educational Series, 2000.** Tips on utilizing dozens of online job-search links, detailed advice for locating targeted jobs, and more than 100 model resumes and cover letters dedicated to business management and professional positions.

Wilson, Robert F., *Conducting Better Job Interviews, 2nd ed.* **Hauppauge, N.Y.: Barron's, 1997.** Secrets from the employer's side of the desk. What new managers are taught about how to choose the best person for the job. Includes organizational priorities, testing and screening, evaluating resumes, and structuring a win-win selection interview.

Wilson, Robert F., *Interview to Win, 2nd ed.* **(video, 32 min., color). Saxtons River, Vt.: Wilson McLeran, Inc., 2000.** Covers such executive-level interviewing concerns as The First Impression, Defining the Job, The Ideal Candidate, Overcoming Objections, and Negotiating Compensation. Based on an award-winning career transition program used by corporations nationwide.

Zinsser, William, *On Writing Well.* **New York: HarperCollins Publishers, 2001.** Sound advice for anyone utilizing written communication on a daily basis. Dozens of examples of good writing, buttressed by sound analysis and practical advice.

Index

About the Author

R**obert F. Wilson** has specialized in career management for more than 20 years as a workshop leader, executive search consultant, outplacement counselor, and contributor to Internet resource providers. He is president of Wilson McLeran, Inc., in Saxtons River, Vermont. Wilson is the author of the award-winning career transition program *Job-Bridge* and the writer and producer of job-search videotapes, among them *Interview to Win* and *Interview to Win Your First Job*. His previous books include *The Dot-Com Decision, Your Career in Healthcare, Better Résumés for Executives and Professionals, Conducting Better Job Interviews,* and *Success Without College: Careers in Sports, Fitness, and Recreation.*